You Are the Mom

Stirring Faith, Adding Grace,
and Pouring the Love of Jesus into Our Families

A 40-DAY DEVOTIONAL

Laurie Devernoe

You Are the Mom

Stirring Faith, Adding Grace, and Pouring the Love of Jesus into Our Families

A 40-Day Devotional

Published by Laurie Devernoe • Troy, New York

www.lauriedevernoe.com

ISBN: 978-1-7379976-4-1

CONTENTS

A NOTE BEFORE YOU BEGIN

When I think of the hands that may hold this book, I think of hands that have cared for the precious children who change our worlds. I think of the laughter and tears that go into parenting. The exhaustion and the fear, the wonder and the awe. I think of how selfless you have become to mother your children.

And when I say children, I am not referring only to those you carry in your womb — but also those you carry in your heart. The adopted children, the stepchildren, the blended families. I think of those who may sit at your counter or ride in your car, the ones who simply need the touch of a mother. You are their mom too.

My first encounter with motherhood was in a doctor's appointment when I was sent for an emergency ultrasound. I was familiar with this new round of symptoms I previously had that landed with a miscarriage. As I lay on the cold exam table, I wondered if I was even pregnant again.

The ultrasound tech began asking questions I wasn't prepared for. Do you use fertility drugs? No. Do you mind if I call more people in to look at this? I stammered something. More technicians filed into the room. The discomfort grew — the cold table, the lack of privacy. The growing sense that something significant was happening that nobody was explaining to me yet. I kept asking if everything was okay. Nobody answered directly.

And then the tech — a complete stranger — spoke four words that changed my life:

"We see three heartbeats."

A few months later my husband and I drove home from the gender reveal in complete silence. Three girls — I was terrified. What if they all turned out like me? Then I reasoned with myself — they don't start as teenagers. I'll have a little time to work with them.

Eighteen months after Rachael, Rebecca, and Sarah were born, my oldest son Ronnie Jr. arrived and fit right into the toddler circus without missing a beat. Eight years later — and five pregnancy tests, because I was in denial — Caleb was born. He was thrown immediately into the mix of baseball, travel baseball, softball, music practices, lessons, performances and church culture. Most of his infant time was spent in the car. He hated it.

My kids changed me. They gave me the courage to fight for things I never would have fought for on my own. And somewhere along the way, they became my best friends. I'm grateful for every chaotic, beautiful, impossible mile of this journey. If anything our family figured out along the way can help you build yours — I'm glad to pass it on.

The role of a mom doesn't mean we are perfect. You may have forgotten lunches, been late to meetings, and hoped no one would notice that your daughter wore a bathing suit to dance class because you couldn't find her leotard. You have mopped up messes holding your breath so you didn't gag. You have used creativity you didn't know you had to pull together a project at the last minute when it was too late to get to the store for supplies.

But you showed up. You didn't wait to feel like it — you just kept showing up. You sacrifice your time, the time you could invest in your marriage or the gym, the time you could have used to build a stronger career. But you take what you can get, because you are committed to those three letters: M-O-M. In whatever form you answer to that word — Mum, Madre, Ma, Mommy, or even Bruh (moms of teen boys know what I'm talking about) — you show up.

So when you hold this book and read these words, I am writing to you. To the exhausted you. To the scared you. To the you who wonders if anyone else feels as clueless as you do — yes. Yes, we do.

By the time you reach the last page, I hope you will put this book down and let me take your hands — the hands that held the cup of your warm, or maybe lukewarm coffee, depending on the season of parenting you are currently in — and let me look you in the eyes and say, with tears in mine: You. You are the mom your child needs. And you are enough.

As women of faith, we carry a particular kind of pressure. Church attendance. Youth group. Bible study. A faith that gets challenged in more ways than we can keep up with. And maybe you feel your faith just isn't enough right now. To that I would say: take some of mine to get you through. God is the God of the impossible, and raising a family is an impossible task — but He comes alongside us to make something messy turn beautiful. Never perfect. But ours.

This book is written for the mom who never feels like she measures up. Who wonders if her efforts go unseen, if anyone actually hears her voice. She may not have a set time to pray — instead she whispers prayers throughout her day, and especially when she lies in bed at night, exhausted but unable to sleep, hoping her family is okay, will be okay — her mind running through everything she forgot but promises to get done tomorrow.

This book is for the mom who carries it all and still feels like it's never enough. For the mom who won't let her family see her cry. For the mom who is always willing to give up the last piece of dessert so one of her kids can have seconds.

This book is for you.

Laurie
DEVERNOE

HOW TO MOVE THROUGH THE 40 DAYS

This devotional is designed to be simple. One day at a time. That is it.

Each day includes three things: a scripture, a reflection, and a prayer. The scripture gives you something to stand on. The reflection gives you something to sit with. The prayer gives you somewhere to bring it all.

You do not have to read this book in forty consecutive days. Life with children rarely cooperates with a plan that tidy. If you miss a day — or five — you did not fall behind. You just pick up where you left off. There is no guilt here — that's one of the things we will talk about.

You can read it alone in the quiet, if you ever find any. You can read it in the car line, on your lunch break, or in the two minutes before everyone wakes up. Some moms have read books like this in the bathroom with the door locked, and that counts too.

At the end of each day there is a prayer written in the first-person plural — we, not just I — because you are not the only one praying these words. Somewhere, right now, another mom is holding this same book, in her own season, carrying her own weight, whispering the same prayer. You are in good company.

One more thing: do not skip the days that make you uncomfortable. Those are usually the ones written just for you.

CHAPTER ONE

You Are the Mom

On identity, calling, and the irreplaceable role you carry.

Before we talk about what you do as a mom, let's start with who you are. Not your to-do list. Not your track record. Not what you got right today or what you got wrong. You — the one God specifically chose for these specific children. That is where we begin.

DAY 1

I'm the Mom

SCRIPTURE

> **1 John 3:1 (NIV)** *See what great love the Father has lavished on us, that we should be called children of God! And that is what we are!*

REFLECTION

When my triplet daughters were toddlers, our first floor looked like a day care center.

We'd only moved into our house eight weeks before they were born, so we never really got to figure out how we wanted our home to look. We went from moving boxes to newborn supplies — enough to open our own store — and landed squarely in the middle of a toddler circus, bright colors and multiple acts going on all at once. I kept their newborn brother in a bouncy seat on the table nearby, overlooking the room the girls were gated in.

I was constantly on alert. Making sure the forbidden climbing zones stayed clear of curious toddlers. Refereeing the toy stealing. Trying to stay one step ahead of whatever was about to happen next. When the commotion would get to me and I'd feel the weight of it, I'd often say it out loud to myself:

"I'm the Mom."

Part pep talk. Part reality check. Nobody else was going to show up and do this. Nobody else was going to teach these kids to be safe and to get along. It was my job. And as clueless as I felt sometimes, they were all relying on me.

Even when I doubted myself, God didn't.

Do you ever feel that way too?

Maybe your first floor doesn't look like a day care center. Maybe your chaos is a teenager who won't talk to you, or a marriage that is harder than you expected, or a season of parenting that has you questioning everything. The details are different for all of us. But that feeling — you know exactly what I mean.

Here's what I want you to hold onto today: God didn't assign you to your children by accident or chance. He looked at who they are, who they would need, what they would face — and He chose you. Not the finished version — the real one. The one He is still working on.

That is not a small thing. It is the foundation everything else in these forty days is built on. Before we talk about exhaustion or fear — before any of it — we start here. With who you actually are.

These forty days are for you. Not the you that has it together — the you that showed up anyway.

So say it today, even if it feels wobbly. Say it like you mean it.

"I'm the mom." And remember — your kids are exactly where they need to be. With you.

LET'S PRAY

Lord, thank You for another day.

We come to You today and we receive what You say about us — that we are Your children, lavished with love, chosen on purpose for the kids in our care.

For the moments we feel clueless — give us wisdom. When we feel outnumbered and tired, be our strength. When the commotion of daily life makes us question if we're doing any of this right, remind us that You chose us for this — not because we had it together, but because You knew exactly what our kids would need.

Today we declare over every mom reading this: you are the mom. Not by accident. Not by default. By design.

In Jesus' Name!

DAY 2

Fearfully and Wonderfully Made

SCRIPTURE

> **Psalm 139:14 (NIV)** *I praise you because I am fearfully and wonderfully made; your works are wonderful, I know that full well.*

REFLECTION

I grew up as an only child of a single mom.

I never really knew how much I wanted a family until God gave me one. Something came alive in me I hadn't ever recognized before. And suddenly there I was — a woman who had grown up in a house with one parent, where we spent more time like roommates than parent and child — now building something loud and full and bigger than anything I'd had a blueprint for.

I couldn't look back at my own childhood and say "I'll do it like that." I had to learn as I went — season by season, while raising a troop all at once — and trust God with what I didn't know.

The places left empty in our own upbringing don't disqualify us from this role. They make us hungry and aware. They make us intentional. They make us the kind of parent who chooses on purpose, because nothing was handed to us by default.

God knows our history, the families we came from — what was worth carrying forward and what needed to stop with us. You are not a corrected version of your own mother, or the opposite of her. You are fearfully and wonderfully made, exactly as you are, for exactly this family.

The thing that came alive in you when you became a mom? That was God bringing out something He put in you long before you knew it was there.

LET'S PRAY

Lord, thank You for another day.

We thank You that You make no mistakes. You know the families we came from, the wounds we carried into adulthood, the places where we had to figure it out as we went — none of it surprised You. You factored it all in.

Today we declare that we are fearfully and wonderfully made. Not in spite of our stories, but including them. You have used everything.

Where a mom is reading this and carrying shame about her own upbringing, or fear that it will show up in how she parents — we bring that to You right now. Heal what needs healing. Redeem what feels broken. And remind her that the family she is building is a new thing — something You are doing in her, not just through her.

We are Your workmanship. And that is more than enough.

In Jesus' Name!

DAY 3

Stop Comparing, Start Living

SCRIPTURE

> **Galatians 1:10 (NIV)** *Am I now trying to win the approval of human beings, or of God? Or am I trying to please people? If I were still trying to please people, I would not be a servant of Christ.*

REFLECTION

I learned to compare early.

After my parents divorced, I looked at other families and felt the absence. Two parents around the table. Two parents showing up at school events. A wholeness I couldn't name but could absolutely feel was missing. And because I couldn't fix the difference, I tried to model my life from what I observed other people doing.

As moms, we often run our homes like someone is secretly watching and keeping score. We're trying to do everything well and we're exhausted — but we can't figure out why. We're not in tune with ourselves or our families because we've been too busy comparing our lives to everyone else's. The trips the neighbors take, the cars in their driveways, the Instagram reels that make everyone else's life look effortless. And no matter how hard we try, we can't keep up.

If you just recognized yourself in that — you've already taken the first step. Awareness is everything. There's no need to feel bad about it, just make the shift. Instead of planning what you think your family should be doing based on what you see other families do, gather everyone and talk through what your family wants to consider. Research vacation options together when age appropriate. Spend some time figuring out what feels right for your people — not what looks right because of what others do.

Paul's question in Galatians is one worth sitting with: Who are you trying to please?

Because here's the thing — you cannot build a life, or raise a family, while simultaneously auditioning for everyone else's approval. At some point you have to decide whose voice matters most. And if you're someone who believes, the One whose voice matters most already has told you what He thinks of you. Chosen. Loved. Enough.

The approval you are working so hard to earn? You already have it — from the One who actually knows you completely. And that was always enough.

LET'S PRAY

Lord, thank You for another day.

We lay down the time we spend measuring — our homes, our kids, our choices, our lives — against everyone around us. We recognize how much energy comparison costs us and how it was never worth it.

Today we choose Your voice over the noise and we choose to see ourselves through Your eyes instead. Thank you for all we have to give our families. Thank you for the gift of each family member filling our home and sitting at our table.

We pray for our kids — in a world that ranks and rates everything, help them know You love them. May their security come from knowing who they are and that they never have to earn their worth because they are already approved.

We declare we are free from comparison. We live the life God designed specifically for us as a family.

In Jesus' Name!

DAY 4

We Are Children Too

SCRIPTURE

> **Galatians 3:26 (NIV)** *So in Christ Jesus you are all children of God through faith.*

REFLECTION

At some point, without even deciding to, most moms put themselves at the bottom of the list.

It doesn't happen all at once. It happens one small surrender at a time. You eat last. You take the interruption. You push through the exhaustion because they need you and that's just what you do. And slowly, without a formal announcement, you become the person in your own home who gets whatever is left over after everyone else is taken care of.

We tell ourselves it's selfless. And it is, sometimes. But somewhere past selfless is a place that isn't sustainable — where we are running on empty and calling it normal, where we haven't asked for what we need in so long we've forgotten what it feels like.

Here's the truth nobody says enough: if you go down, everyone suffers. That's not guilt — that's just how important you are. God never designed you to live a life of self-neglect in the name of taking care of your family. You need care just like your kids do. You are not just a function in your home. You are a person who needs tending to.

We are moms, yes. But we are also His children. And He doesn't look at us any differently than we look at our own kids when they're running ragged — He wants us to come to Him. Let Him fill us up. Not just in a crisis, not just when we've finally bottomed out, but on an ongoing basis.

You don't have to wait until everything falls apart to let God take care of you. You can come to Him today, right now, exactly as you are.

You are His child. That was true before you became a mom, and it will always be truer than any role you carry.

LET'S PRAY

Lord, thank You for another day.

Today we come to You not as moms — but as Your kids. We put down the lists, the needs, the mental load of everything we're managing for everyone else, and remember that we too are children of God.

We bring the exhaustion we don't talk about. The loneliness that still exists, even in a full house.

We ask that you fill us up. Not so we can immediately get back to doing — but because You love us. Because we are Yours. May we learn to receive from You the way our own children receive from us — openly, without guilt.

We declare today that self-care is not selfish. Receiving is not weakness. Asking for what we need is not failing our families — it is how we stay whole enough to love them well.

Teach us to come to You before the crisis. To recognize our own needs the same way we recognize our children's. And remind us, on the days we forget, that You see us — not just what we do, but who we are.

In Jesus' Name!

DAY 5

God Sees You

SCRIPTURE

> **Genesis 16:13 (NIV)** *She gave this name to the Lord who spoke to her: 'You are the God who sees me,' for she said, 'I have now seen the One who sees me.'*

REFLECTION

These words were spoken by Hagar — a woman who had been used and discarded, and ran into the wilderness alone and pregnant, with nothing but what she could carry. She had no audience. No one to witness what she was going through. And yet God found her there, in the most unseen place of her life, and met her where she was. She was so undone by it that she gave Him a new name: El Roi. The God who sees. Not the God who occasionally glances over. The God who sees — present tense, active, personal. Because being found by God in the place where no one else was looking changed everything for her. It can change everything for you too.

Several of my kids were involved in music from a young age. And if you've ever had a kid in music, you know without me saying another word — there is a whole world of invisible work before they ever take the stage.

The driving to rehearsals. Reminding them to practice at home. Making sure they had the right clothes for the performance — did the dress shoes still fit? Did they have an extra string in case one broke? So many details, all of it invisible to everyone in the audience, except the other parents.

By the time I'd sit down in my seat for a recital, I felt like I was already done. I had delivered my child, performance-ready, to that stage. In my head I was already mentally checking off what came next.

And then they'd start to play.

And something would rise up in me — pride and tears and genuine awe, all at once — because what I was watching was so much bigger than all the details I'd managed to get there. It was never really about the dress shoes or the extra string. It was about building them up to see what they could achieve. And there they were, achieving it.

This is how God works with us. He tends to all the details — the ones we don't even see Him managing — so that we can step into things greater than ourselves. The invisible work was never wasted. Not theirs. Not yours.

God sees every rehearsal you drove to. Every practice you pushed through. Everything you did behind the scenes that nobody clapped for. It all counted. It all counts.

LET'S PRAY

Lord, thank You for another day.

We bring You the invisible work today — the details nobody sees, the behind-the-scenes that never makes the highlight reel. The early mornings, the late nights, the logistics, the worry carried quietly so our kids don't have to carry it.

Remind us that You see it all. Every act of faithful love is recorded with You. None of it is wasted.

And where we have been so focused on delivering our kids to the next thing that we've forgotten to sit down and be in awe of who they're becoming — give us those moments. Let us see the fruit.

We trust You with the details we can't manage. That's where faith lives.

We declare we are seen by God — every sacrifice, every unseen moment, every act of love. Nothing is missed by Him.

In Jesus' Name!

End of Chapter One

CHAPTER TWO

When You're Running on Empty

On exhaustion, strength, and the grace that meets you exactly where you are.

Some mornings you pour your coffee and get so engrossed in meeting everyone else's needs that by the time you get to it, it's lukewarm. Some seasons your needs go last. This chapter is for those seasons. You don't have to pretend you're fine here.

DAY 6

The Laundry Is Unto the Lord

SCRIPTURE

> **1 Corinthians 15:58 (NIV)** *Let nothing move you. Always give yourselves fully to the work of the Lord, because you know that your labor in the Lord is not in vain.*

REFLECTION

Can we talk about white baseball pants?

Because somebody decided that the sport played entirely in the dirt should be played in white pants, and that somebody clearly never did the laundry. Add football to the list. And wrestling. If your child plays a sport, you already know: laundry alone could qualify as an Olympic event.

And that's before you get to the food. The meal planning, the grocery runs, the lunches packed, the snacks that disappear the moment you buy them. The daily rhythm of keeping a family fed and clothed and functional is relentless. Mundane. And in the midst of everything you do, you feel almost entirely invisible — until something is missing, and then somehow it all falls on you.

I know what it feels like to look at that never-ending list and feel completely unseen in it.

I stop looking at what I have to do and start seeing what I get to do. I get to minister to my family every single day. Every load of laundry, every meal, every detail managed behind the scenes — Jesus sees it. He cares for our children. He sees the daily work we do for them.

Scripture reminds us — whatever you do in love for the people in your care, you do for Him. That includes the white pants.

Your labor is not in vain. Not one ordinary, unglamorous, unseen moment of it.

LET'S PRAY

Lord, thank You for another day.

We bring You the mundane today. The laundry and the lunches and the details that never make it onto anyone's highlight reel. The things that have to get done and the fact that we are usually the ones who make sure they do.

Shift our perspective. Where we have just been grinding through our list of obligations, awaken us to the ministry in it. We get to do this. These are our people and we get to love them in the everyday.

Remind us that You see what no one else sees. Every act of faithful, ordinary love is noticed by You. None of it is wasted. None of it is beneath You to care about.

We do this work unto You today.

We declare that the ordinary work of our days is not invisible to God. We do it all unto Him.

In Jesus' Name!

DAY 7

Urgent Grace

SCRIPTURE

> **Hebrews 4:16 (TPT)** *So now we come freely and boldly to where love is enthroned, to receive mercy's kiss and discover the grace we urgently need to strengthen us in our time of weakness.*

REFLECTION

Our kids feel what we're feeling, often before we're even aware of it ourselves.

When mine were very little and couldn't find the words, I noticed their awareness in their behavior. On the days when I was preoccupied — carrying a worry I hadn't said out loud, working through something heavy — they'd get unusually clingy or act out of character. Unsettled. Sleep schedules off. They couldn't tell me what was wrong because they didn't know. They just knew something was off with mom.

When we tell them what's going on — in their words, simply: "Mom is okay. You are okay." — we give them space and permission to put down what was never theirs to carry.

When they got older, they'd come right out and ask: Mom, are you okay? I'd tell them — age-appropriately, honestly — what was going on. Not to burden them. To free them. Because kids are naturally self-referential. If something feels wrong and nobody explains it, they assume it's about them. They blame themselves for things that have nothing to do with them.

A simple, honest word from us frees them from carrying what was never theirs to carry.

This is the grace we urgently need — not just for ourselves, but to pass on. The grace to be honest about what we're carrying. The grace to let our kids see that hard things happen and we bring them to God. The grace to show them, in real time, what it looks like to not carry it alone.

They are watching us more than we know. Let's show them where we go when we need help.

LET'S PRAY

Lord, thank You for another day.

We come to You boldly today, the way Your word invites us to— not because we have it together, but because You are where we go when we don't.

We bring our kids to You. The ones who are watching us right now, picking up on things we haven't said out loud. Give us the wisdom to know when to name what we're carrying so they don't take it on as theirs.

We bring our own hearts too. The worries we haven't voiced. The weight we've been managing quietly. We lay it down right here.

Teach us to model this for our kids — that when life is hard, we don't disappear into it alone. We come to You — and as we do, we receive the grace we need.

We declare that His grace meets us in every urgent, imperfect, overwhelmed moment. Grace is always enough.

In Jesus' Name!

DAY 8

Without Faith

SCRIPTURE

> **Hebrews 11:6 (KJV)** *But without faith it is impossible to please him: for he that cometh to God must believe that he is, and that he is a rewarder of them that diligently seek him.*

REFLECTION

There is a particular kind of helplessness that only a mother knows — watching your child go through something hard and being completely unable to change it or take it away.

I remember standing in the middle of that with one of my daughters more than once. She was struggling in a way that broke my heart. Part of me wanted to protest what was happening and demand a different outcome. But that wasn't going to help anyone. Especially not her. Being the adult meant setting aside what I wanted to do and focusing on what she actually needed.

She didn't need me to fix her problem. What I could do was pray, not only for her, but with her.

So I grabbed her hands and we bowed our heads. Together, we turned our hearts to the One who could actually help.

That moment — choosing faith in the middle of something I could not resolve — did something in both of us. In her, it planted a memory: when life becomes challenging, this is where we go. For me, I reminded myself that just because I feel helpless in a situation, doesn't mean the situation itself is hopeless. This is where faith comes in.

That is what I had to learn to let go of — the need to fix. When we fix everything our kids go through, we unintentionally take away their opportunity to call on God and learn what faith actually feels like.

So when the impossible situations arise, acknowledge the pain your child is in and take their hands in yours to direct their faith to God in prayer. These are the moments that train our kids to exercise faith in hard times. Not our words about faith — our actions in the middle of the hard thing.

We may not be able to take their pain away. But we can show them how to walk by faith.

LET'S PRAY

Lord, thank You for another day.

We come to You today with the situations we cannot fix. We lift up our children who are struggling in ways that we can't fix for them.

Remind us that faith is not passive — it is the most active thing we can do. Choosing to believe You are who You say You are, in the middle of something that feels impossible to change. That is faith. And it moves mountains.

Help us pray with our children, not just for them. And in doing so, to guide them to You.

We declare that we will not stress about the things we can't fix, but use them as opportunities to cry out to You in faith.

In Jesus' Name!

DAY 9

Ask for Wisdom

SCRIPTURE

> **James 1:5 (TPT)** *And if anyone longs to be wise, ask God for wisdom and he will give it! He won't see your lack of wisdom as an opportunity to scold you over your failures; he will overwhelm you with his generous supply of wisdom.*

REFLECTION

Does babysitting count as experience toward motherhood?

What about having siblings growing up?

I had neither. My parenting began with triplets, and then a fourth child eighteen months later. I was completely clueless.

So I asked God — constantly. Every time I didn't know what to do — which was often — I went to God with it. Not in eloquent prayer. More like, "I have no idea what I'm doing right now and I need help." And He met me there. Every time.

James says that when you ask God for wisdom, He gives it generously — and He won't use your lack of wisdom as an opportunity to shame you for it. That verse was written for me. And I think it was written for you too.

Your inexperience is not an obstacle to God. It is an invitation for Him to show up.

LET'S PRAY

Lord, thank You for another day.

We come to You today and we ask for wisdom. Not because we have exhausted every other option, but because You are the best first option. You know our kids better than we do. You know what they need, what they're ready for, what words will reach them and what won't.

We bring the situations where we genuinely don't know what to do. The parenting moments that didn't come with instructions. The kids who confuse us, the seasons that stretch us, the decisions that keep us up at night.

Thank You that You don't hold our lack against us. You are generous with wisdom. You are patient with our learning. You meet us exactly where we are.

We choose to ask today instead of just pushing through on our own.

We declare wisdom is ours. God gives it generously and we walk in it today.

In Jesus' Name!

DAY 10

He Daily Bears Our Burdens

SCRIPTURE

> **Psalm 68:19 (NIV)** *Praise be to the Lord, to God our Savior, who daily bears our burdens.*

REFLECTION

I used to tell myself I'd rest when things slowed down.

"I'll schedule some time for me when summer comes." "I'll book that appointment after the holidays." Season after season, I kept making the same quiet promise to myself and then finding a reason it still wasn't the right time.

The truth is that the needs of my family never slow down. There is always a next thing. A next season. A next reason to keep going. And because I kept waiting for a natural stopping point that never came, I was just... always on.

Think about it this way: if you went to a job every day, you would have a start time and an end time. Lunch breaks. Vacation days. Sick leave. The job would not follow you into your bedroom at midnight.

Motherhood doesn't come with that structure built in. Which means we have to build it ourselves. And most of us don't — because it feels selfish. Or because we genuinely can't figure out when later actually is.

We were not made to always be on. Rest is not a reward for finishing. Rest is care.

God bears our burdens daily. Not just in the crisis moments — every single day He is carrying what we were never designed to carry alone. You can give yourself permission to let Him. And then let yourself rest.

LET'S PRAY

Lord, thank You for another day.

We bring You the weight we have been carrying. The mental load, the emotional load, the physical exhaustion of being the person everyone in our house relies on.

Forgive us for the times we have treated rest like a luxury we haven't earned yet. You built rest into creation from the beginning. It was never an afterthought. It was always part of the design.

We declare today that rest is not selfish and stopping is not failing. We give ourselves permission to take care of ourselves — it is how we stay whole enough to take care of everyone else.

Show each mom reading this what rest actually looks like for her in this season. Not a fantasy vacation, but a real, sustainable practice of putting things down. Because You bear our burdens every day, and You invite us to let You.

In Jesus' Name!

End of Chapter Two

CHAPTER THREE

Fear Has No Place Here

On overcoming fear, anxiety, and the voice that tries to run your home.

Fear shows up in a lot of costumes. Sometimes it looks like worry. Sometimes it looks like control. Sometimes it looks like snapping at your kids over something small because something bigger is sitting heavy on you. Whatever it looks like in your house — you don't have to allow fear to have the final say.

DAY 11

God Has Not Given Us a Spirit of Fear

SCRIPTURE

> **2 Timothy 1:7 (NKJV)** *For God has not given us a spirit of fear, but of power and of love and of a sound mind.*

REFLECTION

We had finally squeezed in a family vacation — a mini one, but still, a vacation nonetheless.

After a three-hour car ride, we pulled into the parking lot of a well-known aquarium in Connecticut. I had researched, planned, and made the hotel reservations. I was ready.

My four teenage kids got out of the car, looked at the outdoor pricing board, and looked back at me. Not interested. My youngest — the elementary schooler I thought would love every sea creature in the place — was quick to add his protest to the pile — fully outnumbering me while my husband looked on.

And I lost it. A full-blown fit, right there in the parking lot.

How could they? After everything I had done to plan this.

I sat in the car alone for a few minutes. In that moment I had a choice — keep the fit going, or deal with what happened and find a way to move forward. I remembered reading about the Mystic Seaport nearby. We drove over, got checked in, and every single one of us had a wonderful afternoon.

Fear of failing my family rose up the moment they pushed back. So when my plan didn't work, the fear came out as anger. That's what fear does when it has nowhere honest to go. It disguises itself. It hides in our frustration and need for control. Anger may have been my reaction, but the fear I felt caused it.

God has not given us a spirit of fear. He has given us power — the power to pivot, to choose differently, to be the adult in the room even when we'd rather throw a fit. He has given us love — which looks like choosing the people over the plan. And He has given us a sound mind — which is the thing that kicked in when I sat in that car and thought: there has to be another way.

Fear will always try to drive. Let power, love, and a sound mind take the wheel instead.

LET'S PRAY

Lord, thank You for another day.

Fear comes knocking at our door in so many different ways — but You are not only aware of every single one, You are bigger than them all.

We bring the fear that disguises itself as control and comes out as anger. We bring the fear of failing our families, and of not being enough, to You.

We receive what You have actually given us today — power, love, and a sound mind. Help us to lead from those things instead of from fear.

And when we blow it — because we will — remind us that there is always another way forward. You are never out of options.

No fear lives here.

We declare we will not be governed by fear. God has given us power, love, and a sound mind.

In Jesus' Name!

DAY 12

Do Not Be Afraid

SCRIPTURE

> **Deuteronomy 31:8 (NIV)** *The Lord himself goes before you and will be with you; he will never leave you nor forsake you. Do not be afraid; do not be discouraged.*

REFLECTION

After my fifth child was born, something in me came undone.

It wasn't one crisis. It was a season — long, dark, and relentless. A series of painful breast infections that wouldn't quit. Sleepless nights that turned into sleepless weeks. And somewhere in the exhaustion, a list of mom failures I'd been carrying for years got very loud. Mistakes I'd made as a mother started replaying, wearing a groove in my soul that I couldn't seem to get out of.

After the kids were asleep, unable to rest from the physical pain, I'd take out their markers to color what the pain felt like. Rainbows of color emerged night after night as I tried to get the anguish out of my body and onto the page. Coloring turned into journaling, and as the process unfolded, the pain decreased until my soul connected with the truth — I didn't need to be afraid of having another child to raise. The mistakes I had made as a mom did not disqualify me from what was ahead.

It was a season of transition, and I was unable to fully adapt to the new addition to our family until I had settled some things from my past. This took courage. Not the dramatic kind. The quiet kind. The kind that says: I am going to keep going even though I am undone. I am going to face what I've been avoiding. I am going to trust that God goes before me even in this.

Deuteronomy 31:8 was written for exactly this kind of season. Not the single scary moment — but the long stretch of uncertainty that settles over you and doesn't lift on your timeline. He goes before you. He is with you. He will not leave.

You don't have to have it together to keep going. You just have to keep going.

LET'S PRAY

Lord, thank You for another day.

We lay before You the seasons, not just the moments. The long nights where uncertainty settled in and fear ran deep — the places in our souls we never let anyone see.

Thank You that You go before us. That means there is no place we arrive that You haven't already been. No dark season that surprises You. No undone place in us that makes You look away.

We choose today not to be afraid and not to be discouraged — not because things feel fine, but because You are with us and that is enough to keep us going.

We bring the moms reading this who are in the middle of their long season right now. Remind them they are not alone in the dark.

We declare peace over the areas we feel we have failed our kids. We choose to not let the past define us but to trust You with the future of our family.

In Jesus' Name!

DAY 13

The Battle Is Not Yours

SCRIPTURE

> **2 Chronicles 20:15 (NIV)** *Do not be afraid or discouraged because of this vast army. For the battle is not yours, but God's.*

REFLECTION

The hardest battle I ever fought as a mom wasn't in my house. It was in my own head.

The list started building early. The triplet daughter I couldn't get potty trained until she was four and a half. The toddler I accidentally left in the car in the garage on a summer day after he fell asleep on the way home from swimming. The little one who wandered off into a sea of people at an amusement park while I was busy strapping the triplets into the ride. How about the time when... well, you get the picture.

Every mom has a list like this. The moments we are convinced disqualify us. The replays that come at 2 AM when we are too tired to fight back. The groove worn into our souls from going over the same ground again and again.

That list is a battlefield. One we were never meant to fight alone.

The enemy of our souls knows exactly which failures to replay and when. He knows the ones that sting the most. He knows that a mom convinced she is failing will pull back, go quiet, stop investing — because why bother if the damage is already done?

But the battle is not yours. It never was. God is not looking at your list and agreeing with it. He is looking at you — His child, doing her best, still showing up — and He is fighting for you.

Hand Him the list. It was never meant to be yours to carry.

LET'S PRAY

Lord, thank You for another day.

We bring You the battles happening inside us — the failures on replay that try to tell us we've done too much damage to recover from, and the weight of the moments we wish we could go back and do differently.

We thank You for fighting for us. You are bigger than our lists, bigger than our worst moments, bigger than the groove our failures have worn into our souls.

Help us to hand You what we've been white-knuckling alone. Forgive us where we need forgiveness. Heal us where we need healing. And remind us that You are not finished with us — or our families — yet.

We declare today that the battle is not ours.

The enemy does not get the last word in our homes. You do.

In Jesus' Name!

DAY 14

We Have Authority

SCRIPTURE

> **Luke 10:19 (NIV)** *I have given you authority to trample on snakes and scorpions and to overcome all the power of the enemy; nothing will harm you.*

REFLECTION

When my kids were little, we started reading the Bible together as a family. Age-appropriate Bibles at first — the ones with the pictures and the stories simplified enough for small hands and short attention spans. Family prayer time also became a regular rhythm.

As the kids grew, so did the depth. The picture Bibles gave way to real ones. Family devotions turned into genuine Bible study as they hit their teen years — the kind where questions were asked and wrestled with, where theology got tested out loud in a safe place before it had to hold up in the world.

But my favorite version of our family devotional time was never the planned, scheduled kind. It was the spontaneous ones. Where some of us would be in the car with me and others in another car with my husband, on the way home from games, practices or performances — and we'd call each other and pray together on the way home. Then we'd read scripture from the Bible app. It was a culture that belonged to our family.

One of my daughter's friends shared how her family created a similar rhythm — except they gather together in the mornings to start their day. Both count.

Maybe your version looks different. Maybe it's a bedtime prayer or a verse on the kitchen window. Maybe it's five minutes in the car or a text thread with your kids where you share what you're reading. The form doesn't matter as much as the intention.

Whatever form it takes, the point is to build it. Building this culture in your home is not just a good habit — it is spiritual warfare. The enemy has no foothold where prayer and the Word are already at home. This kind of culture doesn't just happen. It's a decision to steward the spiritual atmosphere of our home intentionally — to make prayer and God's Word so woven into our everyday lives that our kids never have to wonder or be surprised when we turn to the Lord.

This is exactly why we build it on purpose. We have been given authority over our homes. Not to dominate — but to steward. To create an atmosphere where God is welcome, where fear and chaos don't get to set the tone, where our kids grow up knowing that prayer and the Word are woven into the fabric of life.

That authority is yours. Use it on purpose.

LET'S PRAY

Lord, thank You for another day.

We take authority today over the atmosphere of our homes. We invite Your presence into every room and conversation. Help us to build rhythms of prayer and Your Word into the fabric of our family's life. Help us to see where in our day our family can gather together and lean into Bible reading and prayer.

We declare that fear and chaos do not set the tone in our homes. The enemy does not get to plant seeds in our kids' hearts and lives.

In Jesus' Name!

DAY 15

Perfect Love Drives Out Fear

SCRIPTURE

> **1 John 4:18 (NIV)** *There is no fear in love. But perfect love drives out fear, because fear has to do with punishment. The one who fears is not made perfect in love.*

REFLECTION

During the years we homeschooled, I had a habit I am not proud of.

When the kids weren't appreciating the sacrifice I was making to educate them at home — or when I just needed them to cooperate and they weren't — I would point to the school buses going by our house. "Maybe you should all go to school and ride the smelly school bus." "Go to school and eat school lunches." I painted the most convincing horror stories about what public school would be like — all in the hopes that the threat would make them grateful.

Looking back, I can see exactly what was driving that. It wasn't love. It was fear. Fear that I wasn't enough. Fear that my sacrifice wasn't being seen. Fear that I was failing at the thing I had committed to. And fear, when it drives our parenting, always comes out sideways.

Our kids feel the difference. They may not be able to name it — they're kids, not therapists — but they feel it. Parenting that comes from fear creates anxiety in them. Parenting that comes from love creates security. Same house, same rules, same mom. Completely different atmosphere — depending on what's behind it.

Perfect love drives out fear. Not perfect parenting — perfect love. And perfect love isn't something we manufacture. It's something we receive from God and then pass on. We love because He first loved us.

The more we bring our fears to Him, the more His love — not our fear — is what our children actually experience from us.

Let love drive. Not fear. Your kids will feel the difference.

LET'S PRAY

Lord, thank You for another day.

We confess the times we have parented from fear and called it something else. The threats disguised as motivation. The control disguised as protection. The anger that was really just fear with nowhere else to go.

Fill us with Your love today — the kind that drives fear out. Not because we've earned it or have it all together, but because You give it freely and we are choosing to receive it.

We declare over our homes today: perfect love lives here. Fear does not get to set the tone, drive our decisions, or shape how our children experience us.

Where our kids have felt the anxiety of fear-driven parenting, bring healing. It's never too late for love to rewrite the atmosphere.

We love because You first loved us. We parent from that place today.

No fear lives here.

In Jesus' Name!

End of Chapter Three

CHAPTER FOUR

Praying for Your Children

On intercession, persistence, and the prayers only a mother can pray.

We so often forget prayer as a first response — not as a last resort. The prayers of a mother can move mountains even before our children are born to us. I think of Hannah in the Bible, who cried out to God while she struggled with infertility. Her prayers were so intense in the temple, the priest thought she was drunk. She wasn't — she was passionate about crying out to God to fill her barren womb. And He did. She became the mom to one of the greatest prophets in the Old Testament, Samuel.

DAY 16

Jesus Loves Your Children

SCRIPTURE

> **Mark 10:14–16 (NIV)** *Let the little children come to me, and do not hinder them, for the kingdom of God belongs to such as these. And he took the children in his arms, placed his hands on them and blessed them.*

REFLECTION

I once had the opportunity to speak at a maximum-security jail as part of a church outreach. I went along expecting to observe. That was until our associate pastor handed me the microphone in front of a room full of incarcerated men.

Shaking, I heard myself speak from a deep place in me — the place where I remembered wanting to know if my father, who wasn't incarcerated but simply absent from my life, ever even thought of me. I cried out to those men on behalf of their children. I told them that even from behind bars, they could find a way to let their kids know they were loved. I reminded them they didn't have to be perfect to love their children. I told them their love still mattered. Still counted. Still had power.

Then the women came in. And I said it all again, and stepped off the platform to weep and pray with them for their children.

Something changed in me that night.

I went home and most of my kids were asleep. I went to kiss my oldest triplet goodnight. And my own words came back to me: I am good enough, even with all my issues, to really love my kids.

Not just the logistics of love. Not just the getting-it-all-done version. Actually love them.

Jesus stopped everything to bless children — not because their parents were perfect, but because they were His. That's the same love He showed in that jail. The same love He shows us. And the same love He asks us to pass on.

You just have to show up. Jesus handles the rest.

LET'S PRAY

Lord, thank You for another day.

Thank You for choosing us to be our kids' mom. Not a perfect mom — their mom. Today we ask that You bless them. Bless them in the ways only You know how to speak to them, in the language only they understand.

We bring the moms reading this who feel like they have too much history, too many failures to be what their kids need. Remind them that You stopped everything for those children. You still do. And You have given us to each other.

Let our kids know they are loved by us today — not because we performed perfectly, but because we showed up. That is enough. You make it enough.

We declare that Jesus loves our children more than we do — and we trust them into His hands.

In Jesus' Name!

DAY 17

Dedicate Your Children

SCRIPTURE

> **Proverbs 22:6 (TPT)** *Dedicate your children to God and point them in the way that they should go, and the values they've learned from you will be with them for life.*

REFLECTION

Every season, my daughter's orchestra would hand out new music. And every season, without fail, she would cry.

The stack of pages felt impossible to her. Too many notes, too much complexity, too far beyond where she currently was. My husband and I would take turns talking her through it, because one conversation was never enough. We would remind her of music she had said the same thing about before — the impossible pages of music she had previously mastered. We reminded her how the rehearsals, lessons and hours of practice had added up before — until what felt impossible became performance ready.

She tearfully welcomed those talks because she didn't want to quit. She just needed help finding her courage again.

I can't tell you how many times my own words came back to me. I would enter a new season of parenting feeling exactly the way she felt about that new music — overwhelmed by what was in front of me, not sure I had what it took to get through it. And I would need the same reminders I had just given her.

Dedicating our children to God is not a one-time event. It is an ongoing act of pointing them toward who He made them to be, over and over again.

We point them forward. God takes them there. And more often than we expect, they turn around and point us forward too.

LET'S PRAY

Lord, thank You for another day.

We continue to dedicate our children to You. Meet them in the challenges they are facing that feel like too much.

Give us wisdom to know when to encourage them, when to push and when to just be present. Help us to see the gifts You have placed in them even when they can't see it themselves.

We pray for the courage of our kids today — that they would push through the fear of what's in front of them and discover what they are capable of.

And remind us that we are learning right alongside them. That's not weakness — that's the journey.

We declare that they will persevere through all circumstances and accomplish everything You have called them to.

In Jesus' Name!

DAY 18

The Prodigal

SCRIPTURE

> **Luke 15:20 (NIV)** *But while he was still a long way off, his father saw him and was filled with compassion for him; he ran to his son, threw his arms around him and kissed him.*

REFLECTION

We usually tell the prodigal story looking outward — toward the child who wandered, the one we are waiting and praying for to come home. And that version is real and it matters and we will pray for those together before this chapter is over.

But there is another version of this story I lived for years, and I wonder if you've lived it too.

For a long time, without realizing it, I was the prodigal. Not from God — but from my own life. From my own family.

I wanted a family more than I could put into words. As an only child of a single mom, that longing ran deep and quiet and unacknowledged for years. And then I had a family of my own. And instead of embracing this as a gift, I held myself back emotionally because I was terrified that if I got too close, it could be taken from me or that I would ruin it.

Fear can make a prodigal out of anyone. It doesn't always look like running away. Sometimes it looks like staying in the house but keeping your heart at a safe distance.

Like the prodigal son, I came to my senses and realized that the life I was protecting myself from was actually the life I had been given and always wanted. And my family was just waiting for me to connect.

LET'S PRAY

Lord, thank You for another day.

We bring You the wanderers today — the ones only You can reach right now. You love them more than we do, and we ask that You bring them home.

We also bring the places in ourselves where we have been the prodigal — emotionally distant, holding back from the life You have given us, protecting our hearts in ways that have cost us connection with the people we love most.

Help us to return home — to be present, open, and fully connected to our families.

We declare that our families will be healed and whole and all the prodigals — those who've walked away from their faith and those who are simply distant in their hearts — will return home.

Thank You that You run toward us. Every time. Without a list. Without conditions. You just run.

In Jesus' Name!

DAY 19

God's Love Is Enough

SCRIPTURE

> **Romans 8:38–39 (NIV)** *Neither death nor life, neither angels nor demons, neither the present nor the future, nor any powers, neither height nor depth, nor anything else in all creation, will be able to separate us from the love of God that is in Christ Jesus our Lord.*

REFLECTION

My oldest son was eight when my youngest son was born. And suddenly — without anyone meaning for it to happen — he felt displaced.

He was still there. Still loved. Still keeping his schedule and activities. But the attention that had once been his was now being shared, and he felt it. He went from being the baby in the family and suddenly he wasn't. And kids don't always have words for that kind of hurt. It often comes out in their behavior, when they act out in effort to communicate the question in their heart: do you still see me?

I had to become more intentional. I looked for one-on-one drives where it was just us. I stopped in his room between the chaos of running the house just to chat. I learned to ask better questions than "how was your day" — questions that actually opened something real between us.

None of it was dramatic. There was no single repair moment. It was just the slow, quiet, intentional work of making sure he knew he was still seen.

Our kids will go through seasons where they pull away or act out. In those moments, there is a question underneath: is your love for me bigger than this?

We do the same thing with God. As His children, we ask the same question — and His answer never changes. Nothing — not height nor depth, not past nor future, not any choice they make — can separate them from His love.

And that love is working in us and our families even when we can't see it.

Our job is to keep showing up. His job is to finish what He started in them. We can trust Him with that.

LET'S PRAY

Lord, thank You for another day.

We lift our kids to You today — the ones who are thriving, the ones who are struggling, and the ones who have hurt us in ways we are still working through.

Remind us that Your love for them is greater than ours. That You see everything we can't see. That the work You began in them is not finished, no matter what it looks like right now.

Where we have been hurt by our kids' choices, help us to bring that to You instead of carrying it alone. And help us where we have hurt our kids. Give us the grace to keep showing up — not perfectly, but faithfully.

We declare that nothing — nothing — separates our children from Your love. That is the ground we stand on today.

In Jesus' Name!

DAY 20

Pray for Their Gifts

SCRIPTURE

> **Proverbs 18:16 (NKJV)** *A man's gift makes room for him, and brings him before great men.*

REFLECTION

When one of my triplet daughters was eight years old, she started asking to take violin lessons.

I told my husband she only wanted to play because a friend of hers was taking lessons and that her interest in playing would pass. I was too busy to take it seriously. She kept asking anyway. My husband listened when I wouldn't and began researching half-size violins and looking for instructors. Can I tell you — that persistent little girl went on to finish her undergraduate degree as a music performance major. She's played in orchestras and ensembles across our entire tri-city area, at weddings and funerals, church services and concert stages. She now writes songs she streams on music platforms. A gift that has blessed more people than I can count.

She almost missed all of it. Because I wasn't paying attention.

Our kids' gifts don't always arrive with fanfare. Sometimes they show up as a question an eight-year-old keeps asking until someone finally stops and listens. Pray for their gifts — and then pay attention. God will show you what He has placed in them.

LET'S PRAY

Lord, thank You for another day.

We pray today for the gifts You have placed in our children. The ones already visible and the ones still waiting to be discovered. The ones they are afraid to pursue and the ones they haven't even found the words for yet.

Give us eyes to see what You have put in them. Keep us from being too busy, too distracted, or too certain we already know what they need. Help us to not miss the gifts You are trying to reveal in them.

We declare that our kids' gifts will make room for them. That the things You have placed in them will bring them before opportunities only You could open. That their talents will be used for something bigger than any of us can see right now.

Help us to be the mom who notices. Who listens. Who says yes when You are clearly saying yes.

In Jesus' Name!

DAY 21

Pray for Their Faith

SCRIPTURE

> **Deuteronomy 6:5–7 (NIV)** *Love the Lord your God with all your heart and with all your soul and with all your strength. These commandments that I give you today are to be on your hearts. Impress them on your children. Talk about them when you sit at home and when you walk along the road, when you lie down and when you get up.*

REFLECTION

My husband coached our kids' little league team for several years. One afternoon during a game, one of the players went down with an injury on the field.

Girls and boys in baseball uniforms surrounded the injured player, squatting down to pray right there on the field. Faith in action.

That moment didn't happen by accident. It happened because of a culture that had been built — in our home, on that team, by a coach who made his faith visible. When a crisis hit, faith was their first response — it didn't matter where we were.

This is what we are ultimately modeling when we pray with and for our children. Not just their safety or their success or their gifts — though we pray for all of those things. We are praying that faith becomes the thing they reach for on their own. That when situations arise they will be quick to use their faith.

Deuteronomy 6 tells us to impart God's commands on our children — when we sit at home, when we walk along the road, when we lie down, when we get up. To create a culture within our family. In the everyday, repeated, ordinary moments that add up to a faith that holds when life gets hard.

Keep building that culture.

LET'S PRAY

Lord, thank You for another day.

We pray for our kids' faith — that they would recognize and take ownership of it as their own.

Help us to build a culture of faith, not just a list of do's and don'ts. Help us be aware of the moments in the everyday — at the table, in the car, on the way to and from practices and games — where we can exercise faith. May prayer be so woven into the fabric of our family that when situations arise, they know how to respond.

We declare every seed of faith we plant will bloom in its time. We trust You with the harvest.

In Jesus' Name!

End of Chapter Four

CHAPTER FIVE

Building Families That Last

On the building blocks that make a family feel like home.

Think of the moments where people throughout your life have made you feel seen. What about when you feel someone really gets you — where you feel truly known? Our souls soak this up as nourishment. And these are the very tools we use to build our families.

DAY 22

Who Is Building Your House?

SCRIPTURE

> **Psalm 127:1 (NIV)** *Unless the Lord builds the house, the builders labor in vain. Unless the Lord watches over the city, the guards stand watch in vain.*

REFLECTION

My triplet daughters arrived at thirty-two and a half weeks. They were all preemies and went straight into the NICU and stayed there for five weeks.

I pumped breastmilk for them around the clock and had people drive me to the hospital so I could sit, hold and feed my babies. I studied those NICU nurses like my girls' lives depended on it — because they did.

When we finally brought them home, I had a color-coded spreadsheet ready. Each baby had her color. I tracked everything that went in and everything that came out. Visitors made appointments and we lived by the clock. If there was a system to be built, I built it — because that was the only way I knew how to hold it all together.

I didn't know how to raise a family of faith, so we applied what we learned in church to our family. Prayer, Bible reading, praise and worship. All age-appropriate as the kids grew. We just acquired the building blocks and God met us in the building process.

Unless the Lord builds it, all of our effort — the spreadsheets, the systems, the color codes, the sheer willpower of keeping five children alive and thriving — is labor in vain. Not because our effort doesn't matter. But because effort alone was never designed to be the foundation.

The most organized mom in the world still needs God to build what she is building. The most efficient systems still need His hand underneath them. You can run the tightest household on the block and still be standing on sand if He is not the one holding it up.

Let Him build it. That is not a surrender — it is the wisest thing you will ever do.

LET'S PRAY

Lord, thank You for another day.

We bring all the ways we have been building our families to You — running our homes, managing our kids, holding everything together by willpower or organization or sheer determination.

We invite You into every room today. Into the systems and habits. Into the parts of our homes and our families that we have been trying to manage without You. In some ways asking for help feels like admitting we couldn't handle it.

But we can't. Not alone. And You never asked us to.

Build our houses, Lord. Watch over our families. Let our labor be the kind that works with You instead of for You.

We put it all in Your hands today. Every kid, every need, every system we built to feel in control. It's Yours.

We declare that we are building our house on the Lord — and what He builds will stand.

In Jesus' Name!

DAY 23

Known and Loved

SCRIPTURE

> **Jeremiah 1:5 (NIV)** *Before I formed you in the womb I knew you, before you were born I set you apart.*

REFLECTION

When my oldest son was a teenager, I lost it over a situation I felt was taking advantage of him. The outburst was not my finest moment — and in the days after, I wanted to hide from the shame of it. But something unexpected happened. In the car one day, he put his phone down and turned toward me. Just to talk. He kept doing it for weeks — showing up, staying present, choosing conversation when he could have chosen distance. And what I saw in those weeks undid me in the best way. I hadn't just known him all those years. He knew me. He understood why I had reacted the way I did — that I was fighting for him, even if my method was wrong. And looking back, what I was trying to get him to see in that moment? He got it. He just needed time to get there his own way. I had spent years trying to know my son. I didn't realize how well he had come to know me in return.

Being known is not the same as being present. You can be in the same house with your children for their entire childhood and still miss who they actually are.

Knowing them takes intention. It takes asking questions that go past the surface. It takes paying attention to what lights them up and what shuts them down, to how they process hard things and what they need when they're struggling. It takes being curious about them, not just responsible for them.

God knew us before we were born. He formed us intentionally and set us apart on purpose. Our children deserve to be known the same way — not just provided for, but seen. Not just loved in the general sense, but known in the specific one.

They will carry the experience of being truly known by you for the rest of their lives. That is one of the most lasting things you will ever give them.

LET'S PRAY

Lord, thank You for another day.

Give us eyes to truly see our children today — not just their behavior, not just their needs, but who they actually are. The specific, irreplaceable person You made when You made them.

Show us where we have been present without being attentive. Where we have been responsible without being curious. Where we have been providing without truly knowing.

We pray for every child who has gone unseen — in their own home or anywhere else. Let them find the experience of being truly known. And let us be part of how that happens for our own kids.

Thank You that You know us completely and love us anyway. Let that be the model for how we love our children.

We declare our children are known and loved — by us and by God — exactly as they are.

In Jesus' Name!

DAY 24

The Gift of Presence

SCRIPTURE

> **Deuteronomy 6:6–7 (NIV)** *These commandments that I give you today are to be on your hearts. Impress them on your children. Talk about them when you sit at home and when you walk along the road, when you lie down and when you get up.*

REFLECTION

Some of the most important conversations I ever had with my kids happened in the car.

Not the planned ones. Not the ones where I sat them down with a serious expression and an agenda. The ones that happened on the way somewhere else — on the way home from practice, on the way to school, in the in-between when nobody was performing and nobody was on guard.

We live in a world that has made real connection harder than it has ever been. Moms on phones at the playground. Movie night where the movie plays while everyone scrolls their own device. No boundaries around screens — for the kids or for us. And somewhere in all of it, a generation of mothers is looking for herself in a phone, not realizing she is missing the childhood happening right in front of her. Many of us think we are present because we are physically there. But our kids know the difference between a mom who is there and a mom who is with them.

The car became sacred space for me. Something about being in a car together lowers the defenses — you're not face to face, there's motion and noise and a built-in ending when you arrive. Kids who won't open up in a kitchen will talk freely in a car, because it feels less like an interrogation and more like just being together.

I learned to protect those drives. To put the phone down. To ask a question and then wait — really wait — for the answer, even if it took a few miles to arrive. And because I had a lot of kids, I learned something else too: I would choose which child sat in the front seat. Not because they were in trouble. Because I knew they needed me that week. It was my way of saying — quietly, without making a thing of it — I see you. I chose you today.

The commands of God are meant to be passed on — not in one hour a week in a Sunday School lesson, but in the rhythm of life. When we drive together and eat together. When we celebrate and when we laugh together. In the ordinary parts of life.

Show up for the ordinary. That is where the real conversations live.

LET'S PRAY

Lord, thank You for another day.

Give us ears to really hear our children today. Not just the words but what's underneath them. Help us be their first line of defense to make them feel known and to be taken seriously. Help us to step beyond the busyness of parenting to make sure they know they have someone in their corner who thinks what matters to them actually matters.

We confess the times we half-listened. The times we were already forming our response before they finished talking. The times we changed the subject because we were tired or distracted or just not that interested in what they want to talk about.

Help us to stay in their world a little longer today. To ask one more question. To let them finish. To resist the urge to fix or redirect before we've really heard.

We are building trust today that we will need tomorrow. Let us not take that lightly.

We declare we are fully present to our families — not just physically there, but truly with them.

In Jesus' Name!

DAY 25

Roots and Wings

SCRIPTURE

> **Proverbs 22:6 (NIV)** *Start children off on the way they should go, and even when they are old they will not turn from it.*

REFLECTION

When my first child left for graduate school, I grieved.

Not because anything went wrong. Because everything changed — and the family dynamic I had spent years building was changing in a way I knew was permanent. As much as I love the adult friendships I have with my kids now, I had to mourn the season that was ending before I could receive the one that was beginning. I had watched other parents go through it, so I knew the grief was coming. What surprised me was that I spent more time dreading the transition than actually struggling through it. The anticipation was harder than the arrival.

As the kids began to spread their wings — in the job market, in ministry, in figuring out their lives — something started happening that I didn't expect. People would stop me. Send a text. Find me in a hallway. "Your daughter really has her head on her shoulders." "Your son is so easy to work with — he listens, he follows through." I was always a little surprised that someone would take the time to say those things to me. And I was so grateful — not because it made me feel like a good mom, but because my kids were making a positive impact on people. The roots had traveled further than I could see from my own house.

Roots and wings. That is what we are giving them. Roots deep enough that they know who they are and where they came from — the values, the faith, the family culture that shaped them. And wings strong enough to carry them somewhere we cannot follow.

The letting go is not a failure. It is the point. And the roots you gave them — the ones that formed in the ordinary, repeated moments of family life — go with them wherever the wings take them.

You are building something that will outlast your presence in their daily lives. Build it well. And then trust God with what grows from it.

LET'S PRAY

Lord, thank You for another day.

We bring You the tension of raising kids to leave. The love that wants to hold on and the wisdom that knows we have to let go. Help us to hold both of those things at the same time without collapsing into either.

For the moms who are dreading the leaving before it has even happened — give them grace for that too. The anticipation is its own grief. Let them feel it without shame.

Where we have confused being needed with being important — heal that. Remind us that our value as their mom is not measured by how much they depend on us. It is measured by who they are becoming.

Give us the courage to keep building the roots even when it's hard, and the grace to keep releasing the wings even when it hurts.

We trust You with where they go. You love them more than we do, and You go with them.

We declare deep roots are growing in our children. They will fly with confidence when the time comes.

In Jesus' Name!

DAY 26

The Table

SCRIPTURE

> **Luke 22:14–15 (NIV)** *When the hour came, Jesus and his apostles reclined at the table. And he said to them, 'I have eagerly desired to eat this Passover with you before I suffer.'*

REFLECTION

The family dinner table is one of the hardest things to protect.

Between school activities, work schedules, church commitments and the general chaos of keeping everyone moving in the right direction, the table has a way of becoming a collection point — mail, keys, lunchboxes, the debris of daily life. And even on the evenings when everyone is home at the same time, a sit-down meal can feel like one more complicated thing to pull off.

But let me encourage you anyway.

Even if it's just you and your kids because of schedules or the circumstances of your life — clear the table. Put the devices away. Let the conversation be organic. Talk about the weather, the game, the movie. Ask questions. Show investment. Keep the space special. It doesn't have to be a perfect meal or a perfect mood. Someone will be grumpy. The food won't always be great. Gather anyway.

Because what happens over time — slowly, quietly, without you realizing it — is that you learn each other. Not just the deep things. The small things too. Favorite foods, opinions about movies, what kind of car they think is cool. That texture is what a relationship is actually made of. You can't manufacture it. It accumulates, dinner by dinner, year by year.

Now that several of my kids have grown and gone — though thankfully still local — I endeavor to gather everyone at my table at least once a month. Some months are harder than others. Some months are more frequent. But what I have noticed in those gatherings is a peace in how they connect with each other. They may not talk every day anymore. But the table was a safe place for so long that the safety remained. The habit built something that outlasted the habit itself.

It is never too late to start. And never too early. Eat with your toddlers. Eat with your school-age kids. Eat with your teenagers who would rather be anywhere else. Create the rhythm. You are building something they will carry long after they leave your table.

LET'S PRAY

Lord, thank You for another day.

We thank You for the gift of the table — not just the food, but what happens around it. The small discoveries. The opinions about movies and cars and food that add up, over years, to actually knowing our people.

Help us to protect that space. To clear it — literally and figuratively — from the debris of daily life. To put the devices down and let conversation happen, even when the mood isn't perfect and the meal isn't either.

We pray for the mom who has lost the rhythm of gathering — to busy seasons, to the demands of life pulling everyone in different directions. Remind her it is not too late. One dinner. One cleared table. That is enough to begin again.

And for those of us whose kids have grown and gone — thank You that what was built at the table doesn't leave with them. The safety remains. The connection remains. The habit of belonging to each other remains.

We declare that our families will return to the importance of sitting at the table together — even if it's one annual holiday meal a year.

Let our tables be the place our families always know they can come back to.

In Jesus' Name!

End of Chapter Five

CHAPTER SIX

Peace in the Storm

On trusting God in crisis, uncertainty, and the long dark nights.

Some of what you're carrying right now, you haven't said out loud to anyone. The 2 AM fears. The situation that has no good resolution. The season that has gone on longer than you thought you could hold. This chapter is for that. You are not alone in the dark.

DAY 27

Peace That Floods

SCRIPTURE

> **Philippians 4:7 (NIV)** *And the peace of God, which transcends all understanding, will guard your hearts and your minds in Christ Jesus.*

REFLECTION

Two of my daughters went through a season where they were in and out of the hospital with an illness that didn't have easy answers. I took the night shifts. I slept on the couch in their hospital room — or tried to — and I kept the household running over the phone — texts to my daughters at home, calls with my husband who would come to the hospital to take turns. When we were together we'd go over everything we knew, trying to make decisions for our daughter — what was the right course of action for her body and for her soul. We were parents trying to be wise about things no one had answers or a diagnosis for.

There was peace over us that didn't make sense — which is exactly what Philippians says it would do. Despite the stress of the situation, the seriousness of it or the lack of a clear path to recovery, we had peace. Don't get me wrong, there were moments when fear crashed in like a wave — but every single time things escalated, something steadied me from the inside out that I cannot explain apart from God.

Peace isn't a feeling that enables us to float above the crisis — it is the thing that allows us to function while going through it. To run my home from beside my daughter's hospital bed. To encourage my daughter without falling apart and to have conversations with professionals while showing patience and respect. To go home, connect with my other kids for a little while and to come back, and do it again.

That is what the peace of God actually looks like in a storm. Not the absence of the storm. Not a guarantee where we will get answers. Just a steady, inexplicable, completely unearned ability to keep going — guarded, as Paul says, in your heart and your mind.

Whatever you are watching over right now — whatever couch you are sleeping on, whatever decision you are trying to make at 2 AM with information you don't fully understand — He is not asking you to be unafraid. He is asking you to let His peace do its job.

It transcends understanding. That means it will show up in the places where understanding runs out.

Let it flood in.

LET'S PRAY

Lord, thank You for another day.

We pray for the moms who are in the thick of it right now. The ones sleeping in hospital rooms, making decisions they don't feel qualified to make, holding it together for their kids while they try to find a path forward. We pray for the moms dealing with storms that seem overwhelming and unbearable.

We ask for Your peace — the kind that transcends understanding. Not a peace that makes the situation make sense, but a peace that guards our hearts and minds anyway. The kind that lets us function when we should be falling apart. The kind that steadies our hands for the next hard thing.

Give us wisdom for the decisions in front of us. Help us to communicate with professionals. Help us to think clearly when clarity feels impossible.

And remind us that You are in the room with us — on the couch, in the conversation with the doctor, in the 2 AM silence when the fear tries to come back in.

We declare peace over the storms in our lives and over our families.

Your peace is not fragile. It is not overwhelmed by what overwhelms us. Let it do its job in us today.

In Jesus' Name!

DAY 28

He Calms the Storm

SCRIPTURE

> **Mark 4:37–39 (NIV)** *A furious squall came up, and the waves broke over the boat, so that it was nearly swamped. Jesus was in the stern, sleeping on a cushion. The disciples woke him and said to him, "Teacher, don't you care if we drown?" He got up, rebuked the wind and said to the waves, "Quiet! Be still!" Then the wind died down and it was completely calm.*

REFLECTION

There was a season where everyone in my family seemed to need prayer at once.

Hard things for all of them at the same time. I missed the days when I could fix things. When the problem was a broken toy or a sharing dispute and I was the solution. But my kids had grown, and so had their problems. These were problems I couldn't solve with some glue or a distraction.

When I would sit down to pray, I needed to get rid of the helplessness I felt — and I lacked the prayer plan to do it. The problems were just that, problems with no clear solutions, needs that required divine intervention. All I could manage was to whisper their names as my prayer.

When I think about the disciples in that boat, I remember they weren't weak or inexperienced. They were experienced fishermen who knew what a bad storm looked like. This one was bad enough that even they were convinced they were going to drown. Even when Jesus was in the stern, asleep.

That detail used to unsettle me. It doesn't anymore. I have walked with God long enough to know that His silence is not absence. His stillness is not indifference. Over the years He had shown His faithfulness to our family so many times that it was no longer a question of whether He knew or cared. It was settled. So when things got messy and overwhelming — I wasn't trying to wake Him out of panic. I was reminding myself He was already there.

When I whispered their names, the burden began to lift. Not their circumstances — those didn't change right away. But the weight transferred. That is what He was waiting for.

If all you have today is names — just their names, whispered in His direction — that is enough. He is already in the boat. He has been the whole time.

LET'S PRAY

Lord, thank You for another day.

We come to You today carrying what we cannot fix. The situations we can see clearly enough to worry about but not clearly enough to solve. The kids whose problems have outgrown what a distraction can reach.

We admit we don't always have the words or the plan to get them through, but we trust that You do. Sometimes all we have is their names. So we bring them to You now —

(Say their names)

— because You already know, and because whispering them is a way we can release what we were never meant to carry alone.

Remind us that Your silence is not absence. That You have been in this boat with us the whole time — not sleeping through our crisis, but present in it, waiting for us to stop bailing water long enough to let You speak to the storm.

For the mom today whose prayer feels like nothing more than a name whispered into the quiet — let that be enough. Because it is. You hear it. You are already moving.

We declare that we don't have to have the answers — we just need to go to You, the one who does.

Quiet the storms around our families today, Lord. And quiet the ones inside us too.

In Jesus' Name!

DAY 29

Keep On Believing

SCRIPTURE

> **Mark 5:35–36 (TPT)** *And before he had finished speaking, people arrived from Jairus' house and pushed through the crowd to give Jairus the news: "There's no need to trouble the master any longer — your daughter has died." But Jesus refused to listen to what they were told and said to the Jewish official, "Don't yield to fear. All you need to do is to keep on believing."*

REFLECTION

There is a sentence that has a way of stopping faith in its tracks.

I heard those words more times than I want to count — from doctors, counselors, professionals who had genuinely done their best and had nothing left to offer. Each time the situation was different. Each time the message was the same.

There's nothing more we can do.

The first time you hear it, it lands like a blow. The second time, it lands on a bruise. By the time it arrives from multiple directions about multiple situations, it stops feeling like information and starts feeling like a verdict — one that is specifically designed to make you put your prayers down.

Jairus knew exactly what that weight felt like.

He had already done the hard thing. He had pushed through the crowd, found Jesus, fallen at His feet, and asked for help — publicly, humbly, urgently. He was already mid-belief when the message arrived from his house: your daughter has died. There's no need to trouble the teacher anymore.

Don't bother. It's too late. Nothing more can be done.

Jesus heard the message too. And He refused to let it become the final word.

"Don't yield to fear," He said. Not don't feel it — don't yield to it. Don't let it take the wheel. Don't let what you just heard undo what you already started. "All you need to do is keep on believing."

That instruction is so simple it almost sounds dismissive — until you are the one standing in the moment where everything in you wants to stop. Where the news is bad and the options are gone and the people around you have run out of answers. In that moment, "keep on believing" is not simple at all. It is the hardest possible thing.

Prayers I had put in motion before hearing those words did not expire when the news got worse. God did not stop working because a doctor or professional ran out of options. "Nothing more we can do" is a human sentence. It is not a divine one.

Whatever you were believing for before the last piece of hard news arrived — it is not too late. You don't have to trouble anyone. Just keep on believing.

Jesus is already on His way.

LET'S PRAY

Lord, thank You for another day.

We bring You the situations that have collected "nothing more we can do" from every direction. The ones where the options have run out and the professionals have done their best.

We refuse to let those words be the final word.

We pick back up today the prayers we put down when the news got heavy. We pick them back up and bring them to You again. Not because the situation has changed — but because You haven't.

You said "Don't yield to fear." All we need to do is keep on believing. So today, Lord, that is what we choose.

We declare we won't stop believing. For our children, for our families, for the situations that have gone on longer than we thought we could hold.

You are not out of options. You are not troubled by what has troubled everyone else. And You are already on Your way to whatever we are waiting on.

We will not put our prayers down today.

In Jesus' Name!

DAY 30

God Is Our Refuge

SCRIPTURE

> **Psalm 46:1 (NIV)** *God is our refuge and strength, an ever-present help in trouble.*

REFLECTION

I have a habit I am still working on.

When something is hard — for one of my kids, for someone I love, for my family — my first instinct is to help in any way possible. To figure out what I can do, who I can call, what angle I haven't tried yet. To make myself useful to the situation before the situation gets any worse.

I am a fixer by nature. And for a long time I told myself that was just how I was wired — that it was actually a strength, this ability to stay in motion when things got hard. Life has taught me that it is not always a strength. Sometimes it is a way of avoiding the one thing I actually need to do.

My pattern goes like this: something happens. I mobilize. I overthink, I coordinate, I try to absorb as much of everyone else's difficulty as I possibly can so that the people I love don't have to carry it alone. And then, eventually — sometimes quickly, sometimes after a very long time — the frustration breaks through. Because I was never designed to carry all of it. Nobody is. And the weight of everything I picked up trying to help everyone lands on me all at once, and I wonder why I am so depleted.

Psalm 46 doesn't say God is our refuge when we have tried everything else. It says He is our refuge. Present tense. Ever-present. Not contingent on how depleted we are before we arrive. The refuge is not a reward for the mom who has finally hit her limit — it is the starting place. First. Always. Before we even know how bad it's going to get.

I don't have to earn my way to God by becoming exhausted first.

Neither do you.

God is our refuge and strength. An ever-present help. Not an emergency contact. Not a backup plan.

First. Always. Before we even know how bad it's going to get.

I am still learning to let this truth govern me. But I am learning.

LET'S PRAY

Lord, thank You for another day.

We confess the habit of going to every other place before we come to You. The fixing, the managing, the absorbing of everyone else's difficulty until we are the ones who are broken. We do it because we love our people. But we do it without You, and that was never the design.

Forgive us for treating You like a last resort. For arriving at Your door depleted, frustrated, and empty — when You have been here the whole time, ready to be our refuge from the very beginning.

Teach us to come first. Before we have tried everything else. Before the frustration breaks through. Before we have nothing left. Let this truth govern the way we move through our days — that You are ever-present, that Your strength is available right now, that we do not have to earn our way to You by becoming overwhelmed.

We lay down today what we have been carrying for everyone around us. We bring it to You — our kids, our families, the situations we have been trying to manage in our own strength. We trust You with what we were never designed to hold alone.

You are our refuge. Let us live like we believe that.

We declare God is our first refuge — not our last resort. We run to Him first. Always.

In Jesus' Name!

DAY 31

Show Up For Each Other

SCRIPTURE

> **Romans 12:15 (NIV)** *Rejoice with those who rejoice; mourn with those who mourn.*

REFLECTION

What happens at your house when the board game comes out?

Because in my house, it is never just a game. There is always someone who has quietly decided the rules don't fully apply to them. Someone who argues every call. Someone who takes winning a little too seriously and losing a little too hard. The volume goes up. The competitive streak that nobody knew was in there suddenly makes a full appearance. And somehow, the thing that was supposed to be fun has become a very accurate picture of exactly who everyone is.

That's the thing about family game night. It has a way of showing you your family's dynamics in real time — the tendencies, the patterns, the ways you push each other's buttons without even trying. The beautiful thing is that the dynamics are not a problem to be solved. They uniquely belong to your family.

The same people who press our buttons at the game table are the ones who show up to do life with us. They bring humor when things are tense, an extra set of hands when you need them, and their whole selves when it counts.

That is not a coincidence. That is family.

Within every family there will be seasons. Seasons where one of your kids seems to be winning at everything — the grades, the friendships, the confidence, all of it clicking into place at once. And seasons where another one is in the valley, struggling with something that doesn't have an easy fix, watching from the sidelines while life feels hard and progress feels invisible.

Romans 12:15 doesn't give us a complicated assignment. It gives us two: rejoice with those who rejoice. Mourn with those who mourn. No fixing required. No solving. Just the willingness to be fully present to wherever the people you love actually are — to celebrate the wins without minimizing the hard, and to sit in the hard without rushing toward silver linings.

This chapter has been about peace in the storm — about God showing up in the hospital room, in the 2 AM silence, in the seasons that go on longer than we thought we could hold. And one of the ways He shows up is through the people He put around you. The ones who know exactly how you play the game — and show up anyway.

Your family gets to be that place for each other. Not a perfect place. Not a quiet place. But a place where nobody has to be alone in what they're carrying — and nobody has to celebrate alone either.

That is restoration happening in real time. Not the absence of struggle, but the presence of people who stay.

LET'S PRAY

Lord, thank You for another day.

Thank You for the family You gave us — the loud ones, the competitive ones, the ones who make their own rules. Thank You that our dynamics are uniquely ours, because You made us for each other.

Help us to be a family that stays present in one another's seasons. Where a win for one is a win for all of us. Where a hard season for one means the rest of us move closer, not further away.

Teach us to rejoice together without comparison and to mourn together without rushing past the grief. May we be the safe place for one another when we gather — where our people don't have to manage how they're doing before they walk in the door.

We declare unity in our families and awareness to hold the ups and downs for one another, together.

In Jesus' Name!

End of Chapter Six

CHAPTER SEVEN

Let It Go

On releasing guilt, shame, and the weight we were never meant to carry.

There is a difference between conviction and condemnation. Conviction says: this needs to change. Condemnation says: you are the problem. God deals in conviction. The other voice is not His. This chapter is about learning to tell the difference — and putting down what He never asked you to pick up.

DAY 32

Mom Guilt

SCRIPTURE

> **1 John 3:20 (TPT)** *Whenever our hearts make us feel guilty and remind us of our failures, we know that God is much greater and more merciful than our conscience, and he knows everything there is to know about us.*

REFLECTION

I walked into the gym right on time to pick up Caleb from his program, just like I always do.

He wasn't there.

I looked in the usual spots — where the class meets, where he puts his things. Nothing. I asked a few families leaving if they had seen him. No. I checked the locker room. Nothing. I went to the front desk and asked if anyone knew where Caleb was or if they could find his coach to help me.

And then I checked in with my spirit. In that moment, I actually had peace — a quiet sense that he was okay, that nothing terrible had happened. We had gone over our safety talk recently, and somewhere underneath the searching I knew he was fine.

But then the faces of the staff changed. They looked at each other. They didn't know what to do. And something about watching grown adults stand there helplessly — in a facility where my child was supposed to be — made the fear surge. I heard myself say: shouldn't we do something? Call someone? They just stood there.

I had only my car key. I ran to the parking lot to get my phone and called 911. I was in the middle of filing a report when I walked back in and saw Caleb standing with his coach.

He had been in the coach's office. Talking about a video game.

I told 911 we had him. The gym manager informed me, with some indignation, that they run a secure facility. I told him to get the coach a walkie-talkie for Christmas. And then I went home where my older kids made fun of me for my SWAT team instincts, which honestly I needed so I could settle down.

Can I tell you — in those few minutes of not knowing where my son was — the guilt arrived before I had any evidence that anything was actually wrong.

That's what mom guilt does. It doesn't wait for the facts. It rushes in the moment something feels uncertain and drags every past mistake along with it — as if this moment were simply the latest proof of something you've been afraid was true about you all along. Every mom reading this knows exactly what that feels like.

Scripture says God is greater than our conscience. He knows everything there is to know about us — every mistake, every moment we wish we could redo — and His verdict is mercy — bigger than anything we have done and bigger than what we fear we are.

Mom guilt is loud. But it does not have the authority it pretends to have.

God does. And He says mercy.

LET'S PRAY

Lord, thank You for another day.

We bring You the mom guilt. The guilt that uses one hard moment to drag up the record we keep against ourselves. The guilt that has been so present for so long that we've stopped noticing it as guilt and started accepting it as truth.

We lay it down today. Not because we have been perfect — we haven't. But because You are greater than our conscience, and Your mercy is the final word on who we are, not our worst moments.

Forgive us for the places we have fallen short. And we make an active decision to forgive ourselves for where we have missed it. We receive the mercy that follows — without picking the guilt back up as soon as we set it down.

We declare today that mom guilt does not get to run our homes, govern our decisions, or define our relationships with our kids. You do.

Replace the accusations with truth. Replace the floodgate of past mistakes with the simple, steady reminder that Your mercies are new every morning.

In Jesus' Name!

DAY 33

The Potter's Wheel

SCRIPTURE

> **Isaiah 64:8 (NIV)** *Yet you, Lord, are our Father. We are the clay, you are the potter; we are all the work of your hand.*

REFLECTION

I am a better listener when I am in pain.

My regular devotional time with the Lord changes in seasons of pain. Pain has a way of deepening my dependence — I become more tuned in, more desperate for His presence in a way that the easy seasons don't always produce on their own. We don't need to wait for something difficult to sit with the Lord. Practicing stillness in the quiet creates a soul nourishment that comes from being in His presence — and this needs to be a regular rhythm, not a random response to difficulty.

There have been seasons of crisis and heartache where I have gotten on my knees and cried out from the depths of my soul. Not a composed prayer. Not a quiet devotional moment. A cry. Fix this. Fix me. Take this away. Do it now. The kind of prayer that comes out of you when you have run out of anything more dignified to say.

And God does not remove me from the pain.

He doesn't lift me out of it, doesn't fast-forward me through it, or answer on the timeline I had in mind. What He does instead I would not have chosen — but I could not have found any other way: He becomes my strength inside of it. Present in it. Closer in it, actually, than He ever seemed in the comfortable seasons when I wasn't listening as carefully.

Suffering has a way of doing what we rarely do for ourselves — it forces us to step back and sit in His presence. We resist it at first. But what feels like loss is actually an invitation.

The soul nourishment that happens in that quiet place cannot be manufactured any other way. And it is there, in that stillness, that the real shaping begins.

That is the potter's wheel. The clay doesn't choose when it gets placed there or how long the shaping takes. And it doesn't feel like growth from the inside — it feels like pressure, like confinement, like being held in place when everything in you wants to move. But the Potter knows what He is making. And the resistance we feel is not a sign that something is wrong. It is a sign that something is being formed.

You and I are the work of His hands. In every season of life — including this one.

He is not absent from our pain. He is in it with us, shaping us into something we will not see clearly until we are on the other side of our suffering.

Yield to the Potter. He knows what He is making.

LET'S PRAY

Lord, thank You for another day.

We bring You our pain today — the physical, the emotional, the anguish that comes from loving people deeply in a world that is hard. We don't come with composed requests. Some of us come with a cry and barely an uttering to ask for Your healing touch. We ask for relief. We ask for the pain to lift.

And while we wait — we ask for the grace to yield to the process and to stay on the wheel. We trust that what You are doing in us through this is real and lasting and worth the pressure, even when we cannot see it yet.

Remind us that You are not standing at a distance watching us hurt. You are in it with us. You are the strength we find when we have nothing else left. You are closer in our pain than we ever expected You to be.

We declare: You are the Potter. We are the clay. We trust Your hands today.

In Jesus' Name!

DAY 34

Beauty for Ashes

SCRIPTURE

> **Isaiah 61:3 (NKJV)** *To console those who mourn in Zion, to give them beauty for ashes, the oil of joy for mourning, the garment of praise for the spirit of heaviness; that they may be called trees of righteousness, the planting of the Lord, that He may be glorified.*

REFLECTION

I am so grateful we built family structures when the building was easier.

Not because I was particularly wise about it at the time — mostly because we were just doing what we knew to do. We prayed together. We read the Bible. We went to church. We made these things part of the rhythms of our family life, the way you make dinner part of the routine, or bedtime, or Saturday mornings. Some days we were distracted; some days we sat down together after an argument to pray and read the Bible, wondering if it was okay to do those things when we hadn't gotten along, but we kept showing up and over time this became the framework our family stood on.

I didn't realize what we were building until the hard seasons came and showed me. When trials hit, we didn't have to sort through chaos and confusion trying to figure out what to do. We already knew. As a family of faith, we knew — we prayed together, we stayed in the Word, and when we needed more we asked others in our community of faith to join us. The framework was already there. We had just been building it all along.

Maybe you are reading this and you are just starting out. Maybe faith is new to your family, or the language of building a family of faith feels unfamiliar — like you walked into the middle of a conversation everyone else seems to already know how to have. I want you to hear this clearly: you do not have to have it all figured out to start. The building blocks are simpler than they look.

Pray with your kids — even if it's short, even if it feels awkward at first. Read scripture together — even one verse, even if they squirm. Go to church — even when it would be easier to stay home. Create rhythms that say, in your home, faith is not an add-on. It is the foundation. You are laying something right now that your family will stand on in ways you cannot yet see. The ordinary, repeated acts of showing up to these things are not small — they carry your family, especially when hard seasons come.

Because the hard seasons will come. They come for every family. And when they do — when the accumulation hits and hope gets worn down to something quiet and fragile — what you built in the easy seasons will be what holds.

That is the beauty for ashes. Not that the hard seasons won't cost you — they will. But that God takes what burned and gives back something the fire couldn't touch: a family that learned, through surviving hard things together, that He was faithful. That the building blocks you laid in the quiet seasons were exactly what was needed.

Keep building. Keep praying. Keep gathering your family around the things that hold.

You may not see what you are building until you see the impact of how faith knits your family together. But you will, and it will be there.

LET'S PRAY

Lord, thank You for another day.

We thank You for the building blocks of faith — the prayers, the scripture, the gathering together that holds us when nothing else does. We don't always understand what we are building. We just keep showing up. And You meet us there, every time.

For the mom who is just starting — who doesn't have the language yet, who isn't sure she's doing it right — we pray courage. Remind her that You don't need her to be an expert. You just need her to begin. The small, faithful things she does today are already becoming something.

We place before You the ashes — the losses that left marks, the hard seasons that cost more than we expected. We ask for the exchange You promised — beauty for ashes, the oil of joy for mourning, the garment of praise for the spirit of heaviness.

We trust that what we laid down in the easy seasons is still standing.

We declare today that shame does not define us.

The hard seasons were real — and You were in every one of them, holding what we could not hold, building what we could not see.

In Jesus' Name!

DAY 35

Not by Might

SCRIPTURE

> **Zechariah 4:6 (NIV)** *Not by might nor by power, but by my Spirit, says the Lord Almighty.*

REFLECTION

Caring for the needs of newborns was easier for me than toddlers. In an effort to have some help tying shoes on constantly moving feet, zipping coats for bodies in motion for trips to the grocery store and visits to the park, we hired a mother's helper.

She was in high school and had less life experience than me in most areas.

But she knew children. And I watched her.

One afternoon she was working with my kids on sharing. I observed quietly from nearby, genuinely trying to learn. I'm an only child. Sharing anything was not a part of my skillset. Instead, I tried to buy each child the same toy in a different color. Problem eliminated. No sharing required. Ridiculous, right?! Since I am also linear by nature this seemed like a perfectly reasonable solution.

There was something quietly humbling about being the one who didn't know. I was the mom. I had the experience, the education, the years. And I was sitting in my own living room taking notes from a teenager. That moment did something in me — it loosened something I didn't know I was holding. The need to already have the answers.

I thank God for this young woman who came into our lives when she did. She enriched our family in ways we don't have time or room to describe. God knew, and He provided.

God has a way of putting the right people in front of us at exactly the right time.

Maybe you didn't grow up in a home of faith and you're building something you never had modeled for you. Maybe your family is blended, or loud, or complicated, or nothing like the family you imagined. None of that disqualifies you, nor is it outside of what God can work with.

Zechariah 4:6 was spoken to a man facing an impossible rebuilding task — not with an army, not with resources, but by the Spirit of God. The same principle holds for every family. You are not building in your own might. You don't have to have it all figured out. You don't have to have grown up with the right example. You just have to stay teachable and keep showing up.

The humility to admit what we don't know — to watch, to learn, to ask for help from whoever God puts in front of us — is not a parenting failure. It is the exact posture that makes room for His Spirit to lead.

You don't have to have what it takes. He does. And He is with you.

LET'S PRAY

Lord, thank You for another day.

We confess the quiet feeling that we don't have what it takes — the distance between the parent we want to be and the one we fear we actually are. We have carried that feeling for a long time, sometimes without even naming it.

We bring it to You today and release it. Because You never called us to parent in our own might. You called us to parent by Your Spirit — and Your Spirit is not limited by our experience, our background, our personality, or what we didn't have growing up.

We choose to remain teachable and humble ourselves to learn from whoever You put in front of us. May we be quick to watch and slow to assume we already know the best way.

We pray for every mom who feels like her family doesn't look the way it was supposed to. Remind her that You are not waiting for her to figure it out on her own. You are her strength. You are her wisdom. You go before her into every room, every conversation, every moment she doesn't know how to handle.

Not by might. Not by power. By Your Spirit.

Lead us today, Lord. We are still learning. And we are grateful!

We declare we do not parent in our own strength. Not by might, not by power, but by His Spirit — and His Spirit is enough.

In Jesus' Name!

DAY 36

Double Portion

SCRIPTURE

> **Isaiah 61:7 (NIV)** *Instead of your shame you will receive a double portion, and instead of disgrace you will rejoice in your inheritance. And so you will inherit a double portion in your land, and everlasting joy will be yours.*

REFLECTION

I used to think double portion meant getting back what the hard seasons took — the same things, restored, returned to how they were before.

I don't think that anymore.

The hard seasons don't just take things. They change you. They change what you are able to see, what you are able to receive, what you are able to feel. The mom who has walked through the fire is not the same mom who walked in. And that is not a loss — that is the point.

What God gives back doesn't always look like what was there before. Sometimes it looks like something deeper. A capacity for joy you didn't have before the grief taught you what joy was worth. A gratitude that isn't polite or habitual but visceral — because you know what it cost to still be here, still together, still standing.

The holiday table looks different when you've sat at one with a heart so heavy you could barely speak. The vacation hits differently when everyone can be present in the same place at the same time — something you know not to take for granted. The ordinary moments — dinner, a phone call, everyone finding their way back to the same room — carry a weight of meaning that you couldn't have understood before the hard seasons taught it to you.

That is the double portion. Not a return to before. A deeper capacity — for joy, for gratitude, for love — that was built in the fire and given back as a gift.

And here is what I want the mom who is just beginning to build her family of faith to hold onto: every hard thing you walk through together becomes part of your story. It becomes evidence. Evidence that God was faithful when things were hard. Evidence that the foundation held. Evidence that your family survived something, and that the building blocks you laid — the prayers, the showing up, the refusing to let go — were real and load-bearing and worth every ordinary moment it took to lay them.

Shame does not get the last word. Disgrace does not get the last word. The hard seasons do not get the last word.

Everlasting joy does.

LET'S PRAY

Lord, thank You for another day.

We thank You for the double portion — not the version we imagined, where everything goes back to how it was before, but the real version. The deeper capacity for joy. The gratitude that only comes from knowing what it cost to get here. The bond that was forged in the fire and shows up now in the ordinary moments we no longer take for granted.

For the mom who is still in the middle of it — who cannot yet see what the double portion will look like — we pray that she would hold on. That she would trust that what You are building in her and her family through this season is not a return to before, but something she will not be able to fully receive until she has walked through it.

Thank You that nothing is wasted. Not the grief, not the dread, not the long seasons of wondering if easier was ever coming. You redeemed it all. You are still redeeming it.

We declare everlasting joy is ours. We choose joy!

In Jesus' Name!

End of Chapter Seven

CHAPTER EIGHT

We Are Better Together

On community, encouragement, and the people God places beside us.

No mom was designed to do this alone. The village is not a luxury — it is part of the design. This chapter is a celebration of the people God has placed in your life and an invitation to build your community.

DAY 37

Let's Encourage One Another

SCRIPTURE

> **Romans 1:11–12 (NIV)** *I long to see you so that I may impart to you some spiritual gift to make you strong — that is, that you and I may be mutually encouraged by each other's faith.*

REFLECTION

Remember me sharing with you how I brought in a mother's helper to help with the kids when they were toddlers? We ended up having two teen girls we alternated with as mother's helpers during those years. They came to be an extra set of hands and eyes with my children, and yes, teach them to share because I didn't know how. But while they were there, I was also able to mentor them in their faith. To create safe space for them to navigate their lives while growing as women of faith.

Now, those teenage girls are grown women. They have husbands and children and families of their own. And we are still close — the kind of close that doesn't require constant contact to stay real. Life gets busy, the demands pile up, and we can go stretches without talking. But when we find our way back to each other the bond is still there, warm and immediate, like no time has passed at all.

We laugh now about the memories from those early years — the chaos of the grocery store, the particular challenges of managing triplets plus one (and then two), the lessons we were learning together in real time. And what strikes me when we talk is how those lessons have traveled. The things we worked through together in my kitchen, the things I said on a car ride or over a sink full of dishes — I hear them now in how those women are raising their own children. Something passed between us that neither of us fully understood was happening at the time.

My kids feel it too. These women are not distant memories from their childhood. They are like aunts — people who knew them when they were small and love them still, who carry a piece of their story in a way that few others do.

What's wild is: my neediness made room for it.

I am an only child — self-sufficient, independent, inclined to manage on my own. But I was parenting a troop, and I could not manage all their needs on my own. I needed more than I had, and that space was exactly the opening community needed to come in. And what came in to fill the practical need stayed for something far more meaningful.

Paul wrote that he longed to visit the believers in Rome to strengthen them — and then caught himself. Because it was never going to be one-directional. He would strengthen them, and they would encourage him by each other's faith.

That is how God builds community. Through the need. Through the honest admission that we cannot do this alone — and the willingness to let someone in when they show up.

Your neediness is not a weakness to overcome. It might be exactly the space where your most lasting relationships are waiting to be built.

LET'S PRAY

Lord, thank You for another day.

We thank You for the people You have placed in our lives — the ones who showed up for practical reasons and stayed for meaningful ones. The ones who know our kids, who remember our hardest seasons, who carry a piece of our story that no one else holds.

We pray today for the mom who is trying to do this alone. Who has not yet let anyone in — out of pride, out of exhaustion, out of not knowing who to ask. Show her that the need she is carrying is not a failure. It is an opening to let the right people through it.

Help us to be that kind of person for someone else too. To show up for the practical thing and stay for the meaningful one. To give something to the people around us and receive what they have to give in return.

Help us to build our communities, Lord. Through the needs and the honest admissions that we cannot do this alone.

We declare we are the kind of women who strengthen each other — and who are willing to be strengthened.

In Jesus' Name!

DAY 38

A Prayer for the Single Mom

SCRIPTURE

> **Psalm 68:5 (NIV)** *A father to the fatherless, a defender of widows, is God in his holy dwelling.*

REFLECTION

In those early years of motherhood, I was longing for connection.

I tried different mom groups, looked for my people in different places, but kept coming up just short of the heart-to-heart friendship I was searching for. And then, without any planning on my part, it showed up unexpectedly — the way God's best gifts often do.

A friend of mine watched the kids of a woman she was related to. When my friend would join me for playdates, she'd bring the other kids along. And through those ordinary afternoons — kids running around, snacks on the table, the comfortable chaos of small children doing what small children do — I met their mother.

She was a single mom.

Our families wove together naturally from there. Her kids and mine. Her life and mine, running alongside each other through the seasons that followed. We did a lot of life together — the kind of together that isn't planned or scheduled but just accumulates, day by day, into something real and lasting.

Being that close to her meant I had a front-row seat to what she was actually carrying. Not the surface version. The real version — what it costs to be the only one. To work as hard as she worked and then come home and keep working. To not only provide for her children on one income, but to keep them involved in the extra things like baseball and activities.

I watched her make sacrifices that nobody announced. I watched her push the fear aside — because there was real fear, the quiet, ever-present kind that comes with carrying all of it alone — and keep going anyway. And I watched her reach toward a life for her children that was worth the cost she was paying to build it.

I have thought about her many times since those years, and about the countless women doing exactly what she did — doing it right now, today, without enough recognition and without enough rest. And what I keep wanting to say to them is not advice. It is simply this:

God sees everything you do.

Every sacrifice you make. Every time you push away the fear and get up anyway. Every day you show up to work, come home to your kids, and put yourself last without anyone noticing.

He sees you staying the course when quitting would have been easier. He sees the nights you held it together for them and fell apart after they were asleep. He sees the reaching — toward better, toward more, toward a life for your children that costs you more than anyone around you fully understands.

Thank you. From someone who watched a woman do exactly this, up close, and never forgot what it looked like — thank you.

Thank you for being you. For being the best you can be today, even when today is hard. For being so much more than just a mom — you are their provider, their safe place, their example, their constant. You care, you provide, you make life happen even on the days when it feels like you have no life for yourself.

You are not invisible. You are seen. By your children, even when they don't yet have the words for it. And by a God who calls Himself a father to the fatherless — which means He takes personally everything your children need, and everything you are carrying on their behalf.

You are not alone in this. You never were.

LET'S PRAY

Lord, thank You for another day.

We lift up every single mom reading these words today. The ones doing it completely alone. The ones with some support but still carrying the majority of the weight. The ones who are tired in ways that sleep cannot fix, because the exhaustion runs deeper than rest can reach.

You see them, Lord. Every sacrifice. Every fear pushed aside. Every morning they got up and did it again. Nothing they have done in the quiet and the unseen has been missed by You.

Be their strength today. Be their provision. Be the Father their children need in the places where no one else is filling that role. Step into the practical, emotional, spiritual places — and remind them that they are not as alone as it sometimes feels.

We lift up their children too. Protect them. Provide for them. And grow in them, in Your time, a gratitude and understanding for what their mother has carried on their behalf.

And for those of us who have watched a single mom do this up close — help us be more present, more practical, more willing to show up and stay. Let us be the community she deserves.

We declare her children will rise and call her blessed.

In Jesus' Name!

DAY 39

Sweet Friendships

SCRIPTURE

> **Proverbs 27:9 (TPT)** *Sweet friendships refresh the soul and awaken our hearts with joy, for good friends are like the anointing oil that yields the fragrant incense of God's presence.*

REFLECTION

There is a friend in my life who can tell how I am by the sound of my voice.

Not by what I say. Not by the words I choose or how I frame the situation. Just the sound. She hears me say hello and she already knows — whether I am okay, whether something is heavy, whether I am holding something I haven't yet found the words for. Years of real friendship built that kind of knowing, and there is nothing quite like being known that way.

What she does with that knowing is the gift.

She listens. Not the kind of listening that is really just waiting for a turn to speak — genuine, patient, unhurried listening. She will sit with me through all the details of the story I need to tell, even the parts that circle back on themselves, even the parts that are more about getting it out than making sense of it. She understands that sometimes I don't need a solution. I need to be heard until I am empty.

And when I am empty — when I have said everything I needed to say — she gently guides me back. Not to her opinion of the situation. Not to what she would do. Back to what I long for most: a deep, abiding faith. She knows that is what I actually want underneath everything else, and she is skilled enough and close enough to wait until the moment is right to point me toward it.

I try to be that space for her in return. To see her through eyes of love where comparison doesn't exist. To cheer her on toward more — more courage, more faith, more of who she already is and is still becoming. To hold the mirror steady so she can see herself the way I see her, which is always clearer and kinder than the way she sees herself on a hard day. And to fill whatever space is left with laughter at our shared weaknesses, because that is also part of what makes it sweet.

Proverbs calls this kind of friendship the anointing oil that yields the fragrant incense of God's presence. That is not a small thing. It means that when two women show up for each other this way — fully, honestly, without competition or pretense — something of God is present in that space. The friendship itself becomes sacred ground.

Not every friendship reaches this depth. But every mom needs at least one that does.

If you have her — the one who knows you by the sound of your voice — cherish her. Invest in her. Show up for her the way she shows up for you. That kind of friendship is one of God's most specific gifts, and it deserves to be treated like one.

And if you don't have her yet — pray for her. She is one of the things worth asking for.

LET'S PRAY

Lord, thank You for another day.

We thank You for the gift of sweet friendship — the kind that refreshes the soul, that knows us by the sound of our voice, that listens until we are empty and then points us back to You.

We pray for the friendships in our lives today. The ones already deep — help us to invest in them, to show up for them, to not let the busyness of life slowly starve what took years to build. And the ones still forming — give them room to grow into something real.

For the mom who feels alone today — who does not yet have that person, that space, that friendship that holds — we ask that You bring her one. The right one. The kind of friend who sees her clearly and loves her anyway, who will listen until she is empty and then gently guide her home.

And help us to be that friend to someone. To listen well. To see the people around us through eyes of love where comparison doesn't exist. To fill the spaces between hard conversations with the kind of laughter that heals.

You are present in those friendships, Lord. Let us not take them for granted.

We declare we are the kind of friend we need.

In Jesus' Name!

DAY 40

You Are Surrounded

SCRIPTURE

> **Psalm 139:5 (NIV)** *You hem me in behind and before, and you lay your hand upon me.*

REFLECTION

If we could have done this differently, I would have suggested we meet in person.

Maybe a coffee shop — somewhere with good light and comfortable chairs and drinks that come in ceramic mugs. Or a drive-through on a Tuesday afternoon, windows down, nowhere to be for a few minutes. That's where a lot of the best conversations actually happen. Not the planned ones.

That's what these forty days have felt like to me. A long, honest conversation between two moms who are both still figuring it out.

And this is the last thing I want to say before we go.

Not long ago, my pastor encouraged our congregation to go home and read Psalm 139. I sat down to do it, and I had to stop when I got to verse five.

1 You have searched me, Lord, and you know me. 2 You
know when I sit and when I rise; you perceive my
thoughts from afar. 3 You discern my going out and my
lying down; you are familiar with all my ways. 4 Before a
word is on my tongue you, Lord, know it completely. 5 You
hem me in behind and before, and you lay your hand upon
me.

I read it again. And I began to tear up.

The Hebrew word for hem here is *tsuwr*. It means to bind, to confine, to besiege — to shut in on all sides. The psalmist is painting a picture of being completely surrounded. Not abandoned. Not left to figure it out alone. Surrounded. God behind you and before you, His hand laid upon you.

I want you to sit with this for a moment before you move on. Have you ever felt hemmed in?

I have. The job where I was being treated unfairly and couldn't find the way out. The relationship I was afraid my own choices had destroyed. The long, ongoing, seemingly endless situations where I just needed God to do something — for my sake, for my family's sake, for my relief.

I have felt hemmed in through my helplessness. And every single time — every single time I couldn't escape — my perspective eventually shifted. I stopped staring at the circumstances. And He was there. Showing me something I could not have seen any other way. That He had things under control. That all I needed to do was trust Him.

I don't always remember that well. I want to be honest with you about that, because this is the last page and I'd rather leave you with truth than a performance.

But I keep coming back to something I love to share when I speak to groups of moms. When a baby zebra is born, the mother takes her foal away from the rest of the herd. Just the two of them. Before the world rushes in with its noise and its dangers and its overwhelming amount of everything — the baby needs to memorize its mother. Her stripe pattern. Her scent. The sound of her voice.

That is what being hemmed in is for. It is an invitation to memorize the goodness of God before the next hard thing arrives. So that when the next opportunity to panic comes — and it will come, it always comes — we don't spiral. We recognize the One who has us surrounded. We know His voice. We know His scent. We know His pattern.

So here is my invitation to you as we close these forty days:

Wherever you feel hemmed in right now — in your motherhood, your marriage, your finances, your health, your waiting, your family that doesn't look the way you thought it would — would you sit with Psalm 139 this week? Read it slowly. All of it. Let it land.

You are known completely. You are searched and found and covered. There is nowhere you can go that He is not already there.

You are not trapped. You are surrounded.

There is a difference. And He wants you to know it.

Whatever your family looks like. Whatever season you are in. Whatever you are still waiting on or working through or holding together by faith when the facts don't cooperate yet —

He is behind you. He is before you. His hand is on you.

You are surrounded by a God who knows your name, counts your days, and has never once looked away.

Go be the mom only you can be. He chose you for this on purpose.

LET'S PRAY

Lord, thank You for another day.

We close these forty days with gratitude — for every hard story we told, every prayer we prayed, every truth we picked back up after putting it down. You were in every word of it. You were in every season it came from.

We receive today what Psalm 139 declares over us. That You have searched us and known us. That You are familiar with all our ways. That You hem us in — behind and before — and lay Your hand upon us.

For the mom who finishes this book still in the middle of something hard — remind her that hemmed in is not the same as hopeless. You are there. You have always been there. And You are not finished.

For the mom who finishes this book with more hope than she started with — let her carry it forward. Into her home, her kids, her community. Let what You have done in these forty days multiply.

We are surrounded by You. We are known by You. We are held by You.

We declare: That is enough, because you are more than enough.

In Jesus' Name!

End of Chapter Eight

A FINAL WORD

You made it to Day 40. Forty days of showing up — for your kids, for your faith, and for yourself. That is not a small thing.

As I was thinking about how to close this book, I kept coming back to something my own kids taught me.

Two of my triplets are introverts — often quieter, often overshadowed by their extroverted sister and brothers, especially the youngest, who is an extrovert on steroids. For a long time I thought connecting with my introverts had to look the way it looked with my extroverts — big conversations, shared activities, words. But they kept showing me something different. They didn't need all of that. They just needed me to be there.

When the kids were little, my husband would take all four to the farmers market every Saturday to give me a few hours alone. Looking back, I can't believe I let him — but it tells you everything about how desperate I was. Those Saturday mornings became my Jesus dates. I didn't worry about laundry or dishes. I learned to just sit with Him — often through tears, because I genuinely had no idea what I was doing with all these kids. I tried to read my Bible, but what I found was that the place of real refreshing wasn't in doing. It was in sitting. Just being present with the One who already knew everything I was carrying.

Once the kids got a little older and started expressing they didn't always want to go to the market, one of my daughters found her own quiet way to stay connected with her dad — she just kept going with him. Every week. When I asked my husband what they talked about on those drives, he said: "Not much. She just likes being with me."

That stopped me.

She wasn't going for the conversation. She wasn't going for the activity. She was going for him. His presence was enough.

I think that's what God has been trying to tell us all along. And I think it's what our kids are trying to tell us too.

You don't have to have the right words. You don't have to have the plan or the perfectly executed family rhythm. Sometimes the most powerful thing you can offer is simply this: you showed up. You stayed. You were present.

Presence is ministry.

Go be with your people. And let God be with you.

Laurie
DEVERNOE

Continue the Conversation

MONTHLY NEWSLETTER

Let me encourage you each month with mental health tips and biblical truth to inspire your journey.

www.LaurieDevernoe.com/subscribe

INVITE LAURIE TO SPEAK

As a board-certified mental health coach and sought-after speaker, Laurie brings a transformative, faith-centered perspective to retreats, conferences, and women's ministry events. She helps audiences navigate anxiety, depression, and life's hardest seasons through the lens of biblical truth — offering hope, practical tools, and real-life stories that illuminate God's presence even in the darkest places. Her talks inspire resilience, deepen faith, and leave audiences feeling seen, equipped, and encouraged.

CONNECT WITH LAURIE

www.LaurieDevernoe.com
info@lauriedevernoe.com
Facebook & Instagram: Coffee House Parenting

Laurie
DEVERNOE

ALSO BY LAURIE DEVERNOE

Coffee House Parenting

Stirring Faith, Adding Grace, and Pouring the Love of Jesus Into Our Families

Mom of triplets plus two, Laurie shares a refreshing mix of faith, humor, and real-life insight from her own parenting journey. Through relatable stories and Biblical encouragement, she invites readers to embrace the chaos, find grace in the everyday, and build a meaningful, faith-filled family life.

A L S O   B Y   L A U R I E D E V E R N O E

Seeing Through the Darkness

The Incredible Story of How Losing My Sight Taught Me To See

A powerful memoir chronicling Laurie's journey through vision loss and spiritual awakening. Blending personal storytelling with practical mental health strategies, this book offers hope and tangible tools for individuals and families facing life's most difficult challenges.

Made in the USA
Coppell, TX
07 April 2026

75497596R10063